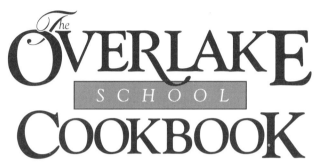

The OVERLAKE SCHOOL COOKBOOK

Edited by
Bonnie Stewart Mickelson

Illustrated by
Casey Lee

Cover Illustration by
Shane Liston

Revised edition published by
Pickle Point Publishing
P.O. Box 4107
Bellevue, Washington 98009

Royalties from the sale of this book will
be contributed to The Overlake School
Scholarship Fund, so that more young
persons of different walks of life may have
the opportunity to benefit from the school's
unique atmosphere that so richly nurtures
personal and academic growth.

Library of Congress Catalog Card
Number 89-063118

ISBN 0-922412-6-1

Book design by Matrix Productions,
Oakland, California

Cover design and illustration by Shane Liston
under direction of Rocket Studios

Printed and bound in the
United States of America

Sixth printing, 1993

The Overlake School Parents Club

is most appreciative of the many who contributed their expertise, labors of love, and favorite recipes to make this a truly special cookbook.

Chairman   Kay Clark
Editor   Bonnie Mickelson
Artist   Casey Lee, Class of 1983

Phyllis Herford   Audrey Salkield
Sharon Swanson   Kathie Wagner
Ginny Coviello   Salli Rogers
            Lori Shepardson

Special acknowledgement is given to Bonnie Stewart Mickelson, known to our community as Bonnie Mikkelsen, a parent of two Overlake School students. She edited the national award-winning Junior League of Palo Alto cookbook, *Private Collection*, and is currently writing and editing *Private Collection II*, as well as producing a monthly column for *Yachtsman* magazine. It is her guidance, expertise, and dedication that have made this cookbook possible.

Contributors

Sada Allen
Walter Andrews
Anna Armstrong
Peggy Ashby
Karen Baggerly
Rosemary Berner
Judi Boa
Beverly Cahill
Mikell Callahan
Joan Carlson
Marilyn Chamberlin
Kay Clark
Darlene Cochran
Ginny Coviello
Ulrike Criminale
Patricia Davis
Dorothy Dike
Susan Drew
Babs Fisher
Ilona Fryer
Jean Harvey
Phyllis Herford
Sharon Johnson
Betty Lou Kapela
Gail Kirkpatrick
Carol Kohoutek
Betsy Lee
Vera Lillig
Mona Belle Lyda
Art Mabbott
Jan McGraw
Jan Mendel
Bonnie Mikkelsen

Christy Oster
Leslie Palmer
Ona Parker
Marcia Paulsell
Angela Peterson
Kathryn Philp
Carol Lee Power
Jonie Pritchard
Julia Reid
Bonnie Robbins
Audrey Salkield
Lori Shepardson
Anne Shorett
Nancy Silvernale
Dot Simonton
Catharyn Spoonamore
Janice Stavig
Alicia Sterling
Sharon Swanson
Karen Taylor
Gloria Thiele
Judy Thomas
Carol Wadsworth
Kathie Wagner
Lyn White
Cathryn Wiley
Patty Winans
David Wright
Sandy Wright
Kevin Wyman
Polly Wyman
Wendy Wyman

Special Friends

Suzanne Beim
Carol Fruit
Linda Grant

Jill Prahm
Beth Ransohoff
Ginny Sproul

Contents

Our intent . . . .

. . . . has been to produce a cookbook that would be an appealing reflection of The Overlake School, a college preparatory school that enhances its dedication to the individual student's personal as well as academic successes through a warm, family-oriented attitude in a delightful setting.

The following recipes were chosen with family tastes in mind, and most are easy to adjust for individual nutritional concerns. Each was carefully tested for quality and ease of preparation; but do note that preparation times do not include interruptions for homework assistance, telephone calls, car pooling, and soccer games! Throughout these pages, Overlake graduate Casey Lee has skillfully illustrated our school's charming rural character.

We so hope that you will enjoy this culmination of many efforts.

The Cookbook Committee

Beverages
and
Appetizers

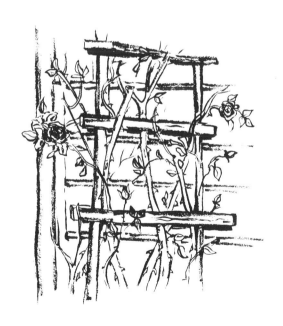

After-School Smoothie

Serves: 1 to 2
Prepare: 5 min.

Fun for the kids to do . . .wonderful for them, wonderful to drink. Use all or some of the following fruits.

¼ cup diced cantaloupe
¼ cup diced watermelon
½ apple, diced
½ ripe banana
½ peach, diced
4 strawberries

1 egg
2 tablespoons honey
½ cup pineapple-
   coconut juice
1 tablespoon protein
   powder (optional)
½ cup crushed ice

Combine selected fruits with remaining ingredients in blender jar. Blend at high speed for 20 seconds.

Fruit Punch with Sherbet

Serves: 30
Prepare: 5 min.

A lovely punch for weddings or garden parties.

  1 pint orange juice
  1 pint pineapple juice
  1 pint fresh lime juice
  Block of ice
  1 quart orange sherbet
  2 quarts ginger ale
  Mint sprigs
  Orange slices

Combine fruit juices and pour over block of ice in punch bowl.
Add orange sherbet and ginger ale, and garnish with mint sprigs
and orange slices.

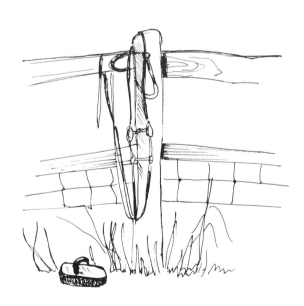

Frozen Daiquiris

Serves: 6   *Keep on hand for special summer cocktails.*
Prepare: 5 min.
Freeze

1 can frozen lime juice
2 cans light rum
3 cans water

Using the lime juice can as a measuring cup, mix above ingredients and freeze. To serve, scoop into sherbet glasses and provide straws or little spoons.

Gin Fizzes

Yield: 4 drinks   *The reason we love Sunday brunches!*
Prepare: 5 min.

1 cup gin
¼ cup heavy cream
4 egg whites
Juice of 2 limes
Juice of 2 lemons

1½–2 tablespoons sugar
  (to taste)
½ teaspoon orange flower
  water (optional)

Whir in electric blender with large handful of ice. Serve immediately.

R. B.'s Famous Eggnog

Yield: 4 quarts
Prepare: 10 min.

One-of-a-kind recipe that will make anyone's holiday memorable!

9 eggs, separated
3½ cups sugar
3 cups bourbon
1½ cups dark rum
½ teaspoon salt

1 cup sugar
1 cup milk
1 quart heavy cream,
  lightly whipped
1 pint peach brandy

In a large bowl, beat egg yolks until thick and lemon-colored. Slowly beat in 3½ cups sugar. Gradually add bourbon and dark rum. Let stand (in large punch bowl, if you wish) while preparing rest.

Beat egg whites until frothy. Gradually beat in salt and 1 cup sugar until very stiff.

With a whisk, stir milk and the lightly whipped cream into egg yolk and liquor mixture. Add brandy. Fold in beaten whites.

If given time, the eggnog may separate. Just reblend with a whisk.

Irish Cheer

Yield: 1½ quarts
Prepare: 5 min.

Every Christmas, our donor centers a beautiful party around this heavenly libation, but you can feature it for after-dinner sipping any special time of the year.

3 eggs
1 tablespoon instant
   coffee granules
1 tablespoon vanilla

2 tablespoons chocolate
   syrup
½ cup Irish whiskey

Whirl the above ingredients for 30 seconds in electric blender, then add the following:

1 14-ounce can Eagle Brand
   sweetened condensed milk
1 pint whipping cream
¾ cup Irish whiskey
½ cup Amaretto liqueur

Blend for two minutes. Pour into your favorite Christmas mugs.

Note: Depending on size of blender, this may have to be done in two batches.

Hot Mulled Wine

Yield: 1½ quarts
Prepare: 5 min.
Steep: 10 min.

Can you think of anything better during or after a blustery day on the Sound?

2 cups water
1 cup sugar
4 cloves
4 sticks cinnamon
2 lemons, sliced
1 ounce brandy
1 bottle burgundy wine

Combine water, sugar, and spices in a large sauce pan. Simmer, uncovered, for 5 minutes. Add lemon slices and let stand 10 minutes. Add brandy and wine; heat slowly.

Smoked Oysters and Cream Cheese

Yield: 1 cup
Prepare: 5 min.

To serve, shape into a ball and sprinkle generously with chopped chives. Surround with attractive crackers or melba toast rounds.

1 3-ounce package cream cheese, softened
4 ounces smoked oysters, chopped
1 tablespoon mayonnaise
1 tablespoon sherry
1 teaspoon onion juice
½ teaspoon paprika
Finely chopped chives

Combine all but chives. Chill until serving time.

Stuffed Snow Peas

Serves: 12 to 16
Prepare: 30 min.

You may create all sorts of good fillings, but the following is pretty, easy, and tasty.

½ pound fresh snow peas (about 48)
3 ¾-ounce cans smoked salmon
1 8-ounce package cream cheese, softened

Boil snow peas in small amount of salted water until barely tender; about 1 minute. Drain and chill immediately by immersing in ice-cold water.

Combine salmon and cream cheese. With sharp knife, slit curved side of pea pods and stuff each with approximately 1 teaspoon of mixture, depending on size of pod. Chill until serving time.

Sesame-Soy Cheese Spread

Serves: 6 to 8　　　*Here's a quickie lifesaver for those spur-of-*
Prepare: 3 min.　　*the moment guests.*

  1　8-ounce package cream
     cheese
Toasted sesame seeds
Soy sauce

Prick holes in cream cheese with a fork and place in shallow bowl. *Generously* sprinkle sesame seeds on top and then pour on soy sauce. Serve with crisp crackers.

Savory Cheese Spread

Serves: 8 to 12　　*The feta cheese gives a lot of "oomph"!*
Prepare: 5 min.
Chill

  2　tablespoons finely
     chopped fresh herbs
     (thyme, summer savory,
     sage, chives, and/or
     dill weed)
  ½　pound feta cheese

  ½　pound cream cheese
  1　tablespoon heavy cream
  1　large clove garlic, pressed
Dash of cayenne pepper
Freshly ground black
    pepper to taste

Hand chop fresh herbs. Process feta cheese in food processor. Add cream cheese and cream; reprocess. Combine with herbs, cayenne pepper, and black pepper. Chill.

    Like a Boursin or Alouette cheese, this is best with bland crackers or melbas.

Six-Layer Liverwurst Appetizer

Serves: 10 to 12
Prepare: 10 min.

Different, easy, and delicious.

8–10 ounces liverwurst or braunschweiger, softened
1 cup sour cream
½ to ¾ cup chopped red onion
½ to ¾ cup sweet pickle relish, drained

8 slices bacon, chopped and fried crisp
1 cup crushed French-fried onions
Melba rounds

Spread liverwurst on a serving plate in a 7 to 8-inch circle. Ice with sour cream, then top with onion and pickle relish. If not serving immediately, invert a bowl over all and chill.

To serve, top with bacon pieces and French-fried onions. Supply melba rounds or French bread.

Sweet and Sour Meatballs

Yield: 2 doz.
Prepare: 25 min.

These are deliciously different from the usual fare.

3 pounds ground beef
1 large onion, grated or finely minced
2 tablespoons chopped parsley
2 tablespoons soy sauce

Juice of ½ lemon
½ teaspoon marjoram
½ teaspoon thyme
3 eggs, lightly beaten
Oil

Gently, but thoroughly, combine above ingredients and form into balls, about 1 inch in diameter (Overworking and pressing will toughen texture.)

In a large, heavy skillet, sauté meatballs in oil over medium-high heat. Do not overcrowd in pan. As each batch is browned, remove with slotted spoon to serving dish or storage bowl.

½ cup sugar
3 tablespoons cornstarch
1 cup vinegar

1½ cups pineapple juice
½ cup soy sauce

In a saucepan, combine above ingredients with a whisk in order given. Heat, stirring constantly, until thickened. Pour over meatballs. These may be served immediately, or refrigerated and reheated in top of a double boiler.

Serve in a chafing dish as an hors d'oeuvres, or with rice for a main course.

Texas Tandy Cheese Circles

Serves: a crowd
Prepare: 15 min.
Chill: 1 hour
Bake 10–15 min.

A very popular cocktail treat, these can be prepared in different fashions. Cut into miniature shapes to be eaten by handfuls, or as 2-inch cookies, topped with a pecan half.

1 cup flour
½ cup butter, softened
2 cups grated sharp
    cheddar cheese
    (room temperature)
1 teaspoon salt
Dash of Worcestershire
    sauce
Dash of Tabasco
Pinch of cayenne pepper
Pecan halves (optional)

Preheat oven to 350°. Mix together all of above, except pecans, blending well. Form into a ball and refrigerate 1 hour.

Roll out to ¼-inch thick. Cut in circles of desired width. Top with pecan halves, if you wish. Bake 10-15 minutes.

Cheese Fondue Cubes

Serves: 12
Prepare: 20 min.
Freeze
Bake: 12–15 min.

There seems to be a number of versions of this, but we think this is the best.

1 loaf French or homemade-
   type bread
½ pound butter, softened
½ cup shredded sharp
   cheddar cheese

1 tablespoon heavy cream
½ teaspoon salt
1 egg white
Paprika

Cut bread into 1-inch cubes (remove crusts only if thick). Place remaining ingredients, except paprika, in blender. When blended smooth, spread on all sides of bread squares.

As squares are finished, sprinkle with paprika and place on foil-lined cookie sheet. Freeze.

Bake, frozen, at 350° for 12–15 minutes, until nicely browned. Serve immediately.

Note: If not using frozen cubes within a day or two, package in plastic bags. When ready to bake, arrange on ungreased or foil-lined baking sheets.

Cocktail Salmon Puffs

Yield: 3 doz.
Prepare: 15 min.
Bake: 25 min.
Assemble: 15 min.

These are fun to make, pretty to serve.

1 cup water
½ cup butter or margarine
1 tablespoon soy sauce

1 cup flour
¼ teaspoon salt
4 eggs

Preheat oven to 400°. Bring water, butter, and soy sauce to boil in a heavy saucepan. With a wooden spoon, stir in flour and salt. Cook and stir until mixture leaves sides of pan and forms a ball. Remove from heat and cool to lukewarm. Add eggs, one at a time, beating well after each addition.

Drop by scant teaspoonfuls on greased baking sheet. Bake at 400° for 25 minutes. Cool.

1 15½-ounce can red
   sockeye salmon, drained
1 cup shredded sharp
   cheddar cheese
1 cup diced celery
¼ cup chopped green
   onion

⅔ cup mayonnaise
¼ cup seafood cocktail
   sauce
½ teaspoon dill weed

Combine above ingredients and refrigerate. Just before serving, split puffs and fill with salmon mixture.

Pickled Trout

Serves: a crowd
Prepare: 15 min.
Simmer: 30 min.
Marinate: overnight
          3 days

Don't let the title discourage you. This is excellent but easy, and is bound to bring raves.

8 pounds nice, fresh rainbows, skinned and filleted
Salt
2 cups vinegar
1 cup water

½ cup sugar
1 tablespoon pickling spices
1 tablespoon salt

Cut up trout into bite-size pieces. Sprinkle generously with salt (about a handful) and place in large, glass bowl. Pack down with a plate, cover, and let soak overnight in refrigerator. Simmer remaining ingredients about 30 minutes. Cool and cover until next day.

2 medium onions, thinly sliced
1 lemon, cut in slivers

Next morning, rinse fish and soak in cold water for 2 hours in refrigerator. Drain and place in a non-metal container such as a crock or the large, glass bowl. Gently stir in vinegar mixture and sliced onion and lemon slivers. If fish is not completely covered with brine, add more vinegar, water, and salt, proportionately. Refrigerate, covered, for 2–3 days, stirring occasionally.

The pickled trout may then be kept in ½-pint jars in refrigerator for ready enjoyment over a period of 2–3 weeks, or may be canned for superb gifts.

To serve, just provide small forks for easy lifting onto crackers or melba toast.

Marinated Mushrooms

Serves: 10 to 12
Prepare: 5 min.
Marinate: overnight

Great with cocktails or for a smörgasbord.

2 pounds fresh mushrooms
  (button-size preferred)
⅔ cup olive oil
⅓ cup white wine vinegar
2 teaspoons chives
1 teaspoon tarragon

1 clove garlic, minced
1 tablespoon lemon juice
½ teaspoon sugar
½ teaspoon salt
½ teaspoon freshly grated
  pepper

If using larger mushrooms, cut into wedges. Place remaining ingredients in a jar, tighten lid and shake well. Pour over raw mushrooms, cover, and marinate overnight. Stir occasionally. Serve with toothpicks. A last minute sprinkling of chopped parsley is a pretty touch.

Stuffed Mushrooms

Prepare: 10 min.
(depending on quantity)

A really easy and good hors d'oeuvre that may be served hot or cold.

Raw mushrooms
Cream cheese
Dried onion
Grated Parmesan cheese
Chopped chives (optional)*

Clean mushrooms and chop stems. Combine chopped stems with cream cheese and dried onion to taste. Mound into mushroom caps and sprinkle with Parmesan cheese.

Broil on a foil-lined cookie sheet until golden and bubbly, but do not overcook. Serve immediately.

*If serving mushrooms raw, substitute chopped chives for the Parmesan cheese. You'll find that the crunchiness of the dried onion is a nice surprise.

Spinach Börek

Serves: 8 or more
Prepare: 30 min.
Bake: 25-30 min.

Walter Andrews, head of the University of Washington's Near-East Language Department, and his family lived in Turkey for several years. While there, he learned how to make Börek . . .by sight, not through a cookbook. We hope that our adaptation of his interpretations has not lessened the authenticity!

1 10-ounce package
  frozen spinach
¼ pound feta cheese
¼ pound butter, melted

2–3 tablespoons milk
½ pound filo dough
  (thawed, but do
  not unwrap)

Preheat oven to 350°. Cook spinach just until thawed. Drain well and chop very fine with cheese. (A food processor is ideal for this.) Combine butter and milk. Set the two mixtures to one side of your work area, along with a soft spatula and a pastry brush. Place wrapped filo dough to other side.

Generously butter a 9×13-inch, shallow, baking dish and place in front of work area. As Walter says, "working with more speed than care," cover bottom of dish with one sheet of dough, folded in half to make two layers. Brush with butter/milk mixture. Repeat until almost half of filo sheets have been used.

Spread on a thin layer of spinach/cheese mixture. Add two more sheets, brushing with butter/milk each time. Spread on rest of spinach/cheese. Finish with rest of filo layers, brushing each with butter/milk.

Bake, uncovered, for 25–30 minutes, or until golden. Serve hot or cold, as an hors d'oeuvre or a meal complement. It can be made in advance and frozen. Allow time to thaw before baking.

Gratin of Artichoke

Serves: 8 to 10
Prepare: 5 min.
Bake: 20 min.

Be sure to serve with buttered, toasted French bread rounds . . .they make the difference.

1 8-ounce can artichoke
    bottoms
1 cup real mayonnaise
1 cup grated Parmesan
    cheese
French bread, thinly
    sliced and buttered

Preheat oven to 350°. Chop artichoke bottoms and combine with mayonnaise and cheese, or blend all in food processor. Turn into ungreased, 1-quart casserole and bake, uncovered, for 20 minutes, until golden and bubbly.

For last 5-7 minutes of baking, place buttered bread rounds on a cookie sheet on rack above casserole to toast.

To serve, surround casserole with toasted rounds, adding a knife for easy spreading.

Sugared Bacon Crisps

Serves: 12
Prepare: 10 min.
Bake: 25 min.

These always go over BIG!

1 pound bacon
1 cup brown sugar

Preheat oven to 325°. Line broiler pan or rimmed cookie sheet with foil. Place 1 or 2 wire racks in pan to fit. Cut pound of bacon in half, crosswise. Separate strips and place on rack, just barely touching. Sprinkle with brown sugar.

Bake 25-30 minutes, until brown and crisp. Do not stack to serve until cool.

Toasted Pumpkin Seeds

Yield: 2 cups
Prepare: 5 min.
Bake: 1 hour plus

Can be roasting while pumpkin carvers are hard at work . . .the aroma will add much to the festivities!

2 cups unwashed pumpkin
   seeds
1½ teaspoons melted butter
1½ teaspoons
   Worcestershire sauce
1¼ teaspoons seasoning
   salt

Preheat oven to 250°. Combine ingredients until seeds are coated. Spread out on large, shallow roasting pan. Bake for at least one hour, preferably more, until seeds are crisp, dry, and toasty, golden brown. Toss occasionally during baking process.

Dips and More Dips

Serve: 8 to 12
Prepare: 10 min.

Although these or variations may be often seen, they are too good not to have again . . . and again. The Flintstone Dip *will be the rage if served in a round, hollowed-out loaf of French or sourdough bread, as described below.*

Flintstone Dip

2 cups mayonnaise
2 cups sour cream
2 teaspoons beaumonde seasoning
2 teaspoons dried parsley flakes
1 tablespoon dried onion flakes

2 2-ounce packages smoked or dried beef, chopped
2 round loaves of French or sourdough bread

Combine all ingredients except bread. Slice a lid from one loaf. Hollow-out insides, cutting into 1-inch cubes, and fill with dip. Place on serving tray and surround with remaining cubes for handy dipping. Cut up second loaf for a ready supply. (This recipe will be so popular that you may wish to double the quantity of dip.)

Spinach Dip

1 10-ounce package frozen chopped spinach, thawed
1 cup sour cream
1 cup mayonnaise
1 1⅝-ounce package Knorr's Swiss vegetable soup mix

1 8-ounce can water chestnuts, drained and chopped
4 green onions, chopped

Squeeze all excess moisture from spinach. Combine with sour cream, mayonnaise, soup mix, and water chestnuts. Sprinkle with chopped green onions. Serve with a pretty assortment of crisp, raw vegetables.

An Exceptional Bean Dip

Serves: 8 to 10   *It's almost too good!*
Prepare: 10 min.
Bake: 15 min.

2 10½-ounce cans Fritos
   bean dip
1 cup sour cream
1 8-ounce package cream
   cheese, softened
1 1¼-ounce package taco
   seasoning mix
20 drops (yes . . .exactly!)
   Tabasco sauce

1 bunch green onions,
   chopped
½ pound sharp cheddar
   cheese, grated
½ pound Monterey jack
   cheese, grated
Tortilla chips

Preheat oven to 350°. With an electric mixer, combine all ingredients except cheddar and jack cheeses. Spoon into a greased, shallow 2-quart casserole. Top with grated cheeses. At this point the dish may be refrigerated until party time.

Bake, uncovered, for 15 minutes or until cheeses are melted. Wrap casserole in gaily colored napkins and serve with a basket of crisp tortilla chips.

Taco Dip

Serves: 12 plus
Prepare: 20 min.

This is similar to Exceptional Bean Dip *and is equally as good, but is served cold instead of hot.*

2 10½-ounce cans Fritos bean dip
3 medium avocados, mashed
1 4-ounce can diced green chilies
2 teaspoons lemon juice
1 cup sour cream
½ cup mayonnaise

1 1¼-ounce package taco seasoning mix
2 large tomatoes, diced
1 bunch green onions, chopped
2 2½-ounce cans sliced black olives
Shredded Monterey jack or cheddar cheese to taste

Spread bean dip in 7×11-inch dish. Combine avocados, chilies, and lemon juice, and spread on beans. Mix sour cream, mayonnaise, and taco seasoning mix. Spread on top. Layer with tomatoes, green onions, and olives. Top with grated cheese. Serve with corn or tortilla chips for heavenly dipping.

Soups,
Sandwiches,
and Salads

Iced Lemon Soup

Serves: 6
Prepare: 15 min.
Chill

This sets just the right mood for summer dinner parties that feature chicken or seafood. Chill your soup cups before filling, then garnish with paper-thin slices of lemon and minced parsley or chives.

2 cups rich chicken broth
1 cup light cream
1 tablespoon cornstarch
3 egg yolks, lightly beaten
Juice of 3–4 lemons
Dash of cayenne pepper
Thin slices of lemon
Minced parsley or chives

In large saucepan, combine chicken broth, cream, and cornstarch with a whisk. Gently heat, stirring constantly, until it begins to thicken, but do not boil.

Pour a little of hot soup into lightly beaten egg yolks, stirring briskly with whisk. Pour egg yolk mixture into rest of soup, continually stirring with whisk. Add juice of 3 to 4 lemons (soup should not be overly tart). Add a dash of cayenne pepper and let soup cool before chilling in refrigerator at least 8 hours.

Gazpacho

Serves: 8
Prepare: 10 min.
Chill

This is definitely not just another gazpacho. The eggs give it a creamy texture to make it different and delicious.

3 tomatoes, unpeeled
1 cucumber, peeled (or ½ English cucumber, unpeeled)
1 medium onion
1 green pepper, seeded
1 clove garlic (optional)
4 eggs

Cut up vegetables into bowl. Place eggs in blender, then add half of vegetables. Puree, then add rest of vegetables and puree until smooth. Return to bowl.

¾ cup tomato or vegetable juice
¼ cup vinegar
¼ cup salad oil
⅛ teaspoon cayenne pepper
⅛ teaspoon salt

Using a whisk, blend above ingredients into pureed vegetables. Chill.

To serve, pour into soup bowls and garnish with any or all of the following: thinly sliced cucumber, chopped green pepper, croutons, minced chives, and bacon bits.

Curried Broccoli Soup

Serves: 4 to 6
Prepare: 20 min.
Chill: 2 to 3 hours

An unusual and sophisticated summer soup that can be dressed up or down. On a hot summer day, serve it for lunch with cheese and crackers, or as the first course at your special dinner party.

2 pounds broccoli
1 cup chicken broth
3 tablespoons butter
2 medium onions, sliced
　 or chopped

1½ teaspoons curry powder
3 cups chicken broth
Sour cream or yogurt
Chopped peanuts

Wash broccoli and trim stems. Detach flowerets and cut stems into 1-inch pieces.

In a large saucepan or Dutch oven, bring 1 cup chicken broth to boil. Add half of the flowerets and simmer, uncovered, until just tender, about 3–4 minutes. Drain, reserving broth. Run broccoli under cold water to stop cooking process. Chill in a plastic bag.

In same pan, melt butter over medium heat and add onion and curry powder. Sauté until onion is limp, then stir in broccoli stems and all 4 cups of broth. Cover and simmer 5–6 minutes, then add uncooked flowerets. Simmer 5 more minutes or until broccoli is tender but not overcooked. Puree in blender in 2–3 batches, until smooth. Cover and chill. To serve, top with chilled flowerets, sour cream, and peanuts.

Note: This is best served within 24 hours.

Mulligatawney Soup

Serves: 12*
Prepare: 20 min.
Cook: 45 min.

Purists might call this "Sengalese Soup", but it's delicious by any name. Serve hot or cold.

1 cup butter
1 large onion, chopped
1 celery stalk, chopped
1 carrot, chopped
2 large, unpeeled apples, cored and chopped

5 tablespoons curry powder
1 cup flour
3 tablespoons tomato paste
2 quarts chicken stock (homemade is the best!)
1 pint heavy cream

Melt butter in large pot and lightly brown onion, celery, and carrot. Add apples and cook until soft. With a whisk, stir in curry powder and flour. Add tomato paste and combine with chicken stock. Simmer, partially covered, 45 minutes.

Cool enough to puree in batches in blender. Whisk in cream. If serving hot, reheat but do not boil. If serving cold, chill 1–2 hours. Either hot or cold, garnish with dollops of lightly salted whipped cream and chopped mint for a glamorous finish.

*Recipe may easily be cut in half.

Albacore Chowder

Serves: 8 to 10
Prepare: 20 min.

A great spur-of-the-moment supper soup.
You'll probably have everything right at hand.

2 tablespoons butter
½–1 cup chopped green
  onions
¼ cup chopped celery
2 cups diced raw potatoes
½ teaspoon thyme,
  crumbled
¼ teaspoon dill weed
1¼ teaspoons salt
¼ teaspoon freshly ground
  pepper
2 tablespoons flour

1 16-ounce can diced
  tomatoes in puree
  (or stewed)
3 cups milk
1 9½-ounce can albacore
  tuna, drained (or any
  left-over fish)
1 cup shredded cheddar or
  jack cheese
2 tablespoons chopped
  parsley

Melt butter in a large pot. Gently sauté onions, celery, and potatoes until tender. Add seasonings and flour, stirring for 1 minute. Stir in tomatoes and simmer another minute or 2. Add milk and tuna. When well-heated but not boiling, then stir in cheese and parsley. When cheese has melted, serve in warmed bowls with crusty bread.

Canadian Cheese Soup

Serves: 6 to 8
Prepare: 20 min.

A neat Sunday supper! Serve with Thomas Bröd.

1 cup chopped onion
1 cup chopped carrot
1 cup chopped celery

½ cup chopped green pepper
3 cups chicken broth

If you have a food processor, the preparation is a breeze. Place chopped vegetables and chicken broth in a large saucepan. Cover and simmer 10 minutes.

8 strips bacon, diced
⅓ cup bacon fat
⅓ cup butter
⅔ cup flour
3 cups milk
1 cup beer

1 pound sharp cheddar cheese, grated
½ cup cream (optional)
Salt and pepper to taste
Chopped parsley

In a Dutch oven or heavy kettle, sauté diced bacon and drain on paper toweling. Reserve ⅓ cup bacon fat in pan and add butter. Over medium heat, stir in flour with a whisk and blend until bubbly and smooth. Add milk and beer, and continue stirring until thickened. Stir in cheese. When melted, add cooked vegetables and broth. If you wish a creamier soup, add a ½ cup of cream. Salt and pepper to taste.

When ready to serve, stir in bacon and sprinkle with chopped parsley.

Italian Oven Cheese Soup

Serves: 4 to 6
Prepare: 15 min.
Bake: 1 hour

A rich, hearty soup; all it needs is hot, crusty French bread. It smells wonderful while cooking.

½ pound zucchini, sliced
2 onions, sliced
1 15-ounce can garbanzo beans, drained
¼ cup butter, cut in pieces
1½ cups dry white wine
1 bay leaf
1 clove garlic, minced
1 teaspoon basil

2 teaspoons salt
¼ teaspoon freshly ground pepper
¼ pound cheddar cheese, grated (1 cup)
¼ pound Romano cheese, grated (1 cup)
1 cup light cream

Preheat oven to 375°. In an ungreased, deep, 3-quart baking dish, combine all ingredients except cheeses and cream. Cover and bake 50 minutes, stirring half way through. Add cheeses, then cream. Bake 10 minutes longer.

The World's Best Turkey Soup

Serves: ?
Prepare: 20–30 min.
Cook: 4 hours+

The pureed vegetables act as a flavorful thickening for this good, good soup.

1 turkey carcass
1 large onion, quartered
4 celery stalks
3 carrots, cut up

1 medium potato, quartered
1 celery stalk
1 onion, quartered

In large soup kettle, place turkey carcass, 1 onion, and 4 celery stalks. Cover with cold water and simmer 4 hours or all day. Cool and strain.

Add remaining vegetables to strained broth. Simmer until all vegetables are soft; about 30 minutes. Remove vegetables to blender and puree with 1 cup of broth. Return to stock.

Onions, carrots, cabbage,
  tomatoes, green beans,
  etc.
1 cup raw rice
Turkey meat, diced
  or shredded

Dill
Thyme
Sherry (optional)
Tabasco
Salt and pepper to taste

For last half hour of cooking, add assorted chopped vegetables to taste, and rice. Cook until just tender. Add any leftover turkey meat and remaining seasonings to taste.

Butter split rolls or rounds of bread, sprinkle with a good salad seasoning such as "Salad Elegance", and lightly toast under broiler . . .that's all you'll need to complete the meal.

California Sandwiches

Serves: 2 to 4
Prepare: 15 min.

You can do almost anything you want with this recipe. Like so many of the sandwich recipes we have included, it's excellent boating fare.

¾ cup grated
   cheddar cheese
1 medium tomato, diced
1 small onion, chopped
2 tablespoons chopped
   green pepper
2 teaspoons vinegar
½ teaspoon salt
¼ teaspoon chili powder
Dash of pepper

Toast and butter 4 English muffin halves. Spread with cheese mixture and broil until bubbly. Serve as open-face sandwiches, or cut in quarters for h'ors d'oeuvres.

Option: Fill hamburger buns; wrap in foil to keep for eating "as is" while boating or to bake at 400° for 15 minutes.

For a speedy hors d'oeuvre, serve just the spread with crackers or vegies.

Tunaburgers

Serves: 6
Prepare: 15 min.
Bake: 15 min.

Very popular with children and can be made hours ahead.

1 9 to 10-ounce can chunk-style tuna, drained
1 cup (¼ pound) shredded cheddar cheese
3 hard-cooked eggs, chopped
3 tablespoons chopped ripe olives
2 tablespoons minced onion
1 tablespoon minced green pepper
2 tablespoons pickle relish
½ cup light mayonnaise
6 hamburger buns

Combine all ingredients except buns. Butter buns, if you're not calorie-conscious, and fill with tuna mixture. Wrap individually in foil and refrigerate until baking time. Bake at 350° for 15 minutes.

Reubens

Serves: 8
Prepare: 15–20 min.

Just in case you had forgotten how good these are!

2 cups drained sauerkraut
1 teaspoon caraway seed
1 loaf Oroweat's Russian rye bread
½ cup Russian dressing
1 pound corned beef, thinly sliced
1 pound Swiss cheese, thinly sliced
Melted butter

Toss sauerkraut with caraway seed. Spread 1 side of 16 slices of bread with Russian dressing. Top 8 slices of bread with corned beef, sauerkraut, cheese, then remaining slices of bread. Brush melted butter on both sides of sandwiches. Grill until cheese is melted.

Jiggs Sandwiches

Yield: 25
Prepare: 30 min.
Bake: 15 min.

Children love these . . .everyone does! A great item for a slumber party, since the girls can pop them in the oven as they wish during the long night.

½ pound butter, softened
½ cup prepared mustard
25 hamburger buns
2½ pounds cooked corned beef, thinly sliced
25 1-ounce slices sharp cheddar cheese
75 thin, lengthwise slices of dill pickle

1½ quarts finely shredded, green cabbage
6 tablespoons salad dressing (sh-hhh! Miracle Whip!)
1 tablespoon caraway seed

Whip butter and mustard until light and fluffy. Spread on cut surfaces of buns; about 1½–2 teaspoons per sandwich. Proportion corned beef slices on bottom halves of buns. On each top half, place a slice of cheese and 3 slices of pickle.

Combine cabbage, salad dressing, and caraway seeds. Put approximately ¼ cup on top of pickles.

Put bun halves together and place each sandwich on a piece of foil so that fold-over will meet at side of bun. (Thus foil can be opened and used to hold sandwich intact while eating.) Tuck in ends and refrigerate.

The sandwiches will keep nicely in refrigerator for a day or so. As needed, bake in foil at 400° for 15–20 minutes, or remove foil to zap in microwave.

Note: For variation, use salami and Swiss cheese and/or substitute French rolls for hamburger buns.

Greek Hero Sandwiches

Serves: 3 to 4
Prepare: 15 min.

We love these for summer suppers or boating menus, and they are a dieter's delight.

¾ pound lean ground lamb or beef
2 teaspoons dried oregano
¼ teaspoon cinnamon
¼ teaspoon nutmeg
1 tablespoon lemon juice
½ cucumber, peeled and diced (do not peel an English cucumber)

1 small tomato, diced
2 tablespoons chopped parsley
Garlic salt and pepper to taste
2–3 pita breads
Tabasco sauce
Plain low-fat yogurt

In a heavy skillet, brown meat in its own juices, adding oregano, cinnamon, and nutmeg while stirring. As soon as pink has left meat, drain any fat, then stir in lemon juice and chopped vegetables *just* until heated. Season to taste with garlic salt and pepper.

Warm pita breads in a 350° oven for a few minutes . . .just long enough to soften. Cut in half and fill with meat mixture. Let your diners dash on a few drops of Tabasco and a spoonful of yogurt.

Matador Rolls

Serves: 4 to 6
Prepare: 20 min.
Bake: 30 min.

When you're looking for something different for your teenagers.

1 pound lean ground beef
1 small onion, chopped
1 clove garlic, minced
1 1½-ounce package
   spaghetti seasoning mix
1 6-ounce can tomato paste
1 16-ounce can corn,
   undrained

1 teaspoon chili powder
½ teaspoon salt
1 teaspoon sugar
¼ cup water
6 French rolls

Preheat oven to 350°. In a heavy skillet, sauté meat, onion, and garlic in meat's own juices. When meat is no longer pink, pour off any fat and add remaining ingredients (except rolls, obviously!). Simmer, uncovered, until excess liquid is gone.

Make a small opening in one end of each roll. Using a table fork, carefully hollow-out rolls, reserving bread for another use. With a teaspoon, completely fill cavities without over-stuffing. Wrap individually in regular-strength foil and bake 30 minutes.

French Bread Pizza

Serves: 4
Prepare: 15 min.
Bake: 15 min.

Teenagers get a kick out of preparing this.

1 8-ounce can tomato sauce
1 6-ounce can tomato paste
1 teaspoon Italian herb
  seasoning
⅓ pound mozzarella
  cheese
⅓ pound cheddar cheese
⅓ pound Monterey jack
  cheese

1 bunch green onions
½ green pepper
¼–½ pound salami or
  pepperoni*
¼–½ pound mushrooms
  (optional)
1 loaf country-style
  French bread

Preheat oven to 450°. In a sauce pan, combine tomato sauce, tomato paste, and seasoning. Simmer a few minutes.

In the meantime, grate or shred cheeses, and thinly slice the green onions, pepper, salami, and mushrooms. Split a wide loaf of French bread in half, lengthwise. Place, split-side-up, on foil-lined cookie sheet. You may have to slice off a portion of crust so that pieces balance.

Spread each half with tomato mixture. Top with cheeses, vegetables, and meats. Bake 15 minutes, or until cheeses are melted and bubbly.

*Pineapple and ham are delicious substitutes.

Sausage Bread

Serves: 4
Prepare: 20 min.
Thaw: 2–3 hours
Bake: 40 min.

A light, family supper that satisfies a pizza craving.

1 1-pound loaf frozen bread dough, thawed
1 11-ounce package "hot" Italian sausage
1 egg, lightly beaten
½ pound mozzarella or Provolone cheese, shredded

Preheat oven to 375°. Remove sausage from casings and crumble into frying pan. Sauté over medium heat for 7–8 minutes. Drain well on paper towels.

With floured rolling pin, flatten thawed dough on ungreased cookie sheet. Press and work with floured hands and rolling pin to form a 10×14-inch rectangle.

Combine cooled sausage and beaten egg. Spread evenly over dough. Sprinkle with shredded cheese.

With floured hands, roll dough toward you as you would a jelly roll. Finish with seams on bottom, tucking ends under and centering on cookie sheet. Brush lightly with oil.

Bake at 375° for 25 minutes. Cut in half, lengthwise, setting halves open-side-up to expose meat and cheese. Bake another 15 minutes. Serve with *Gazpacho* or a tossed salad.

Tabbouli

Serves: 8
Prepare: 20 min.
Soak: 1 hour
Marinate: 8 hours

The allspice makes all the difference! For a tailgate party or picnic or on a boat, skip the forks and roll up the Tabbouli in Bibb or butter lettuce leaves for finger-eating.

1 cup bulgur wheat
2 tomatoes, peeled, seeded and chopped*
1 bunch green onions, finely chopped

½ bunch parsley, finely chopped
¼ cup finely chopped mint leaves

Dressing

6 tablespoons olive oil
¼ cup *fresh* lemon juice

1½ teaspoons allspice
2 teaspoons salt

Wash bulgur wheat, then soak 1 hour in 2 cups boiling water. Place in a cheese cloth or clean towel and press out all water. Combine with chopped vegetables. *(If making a day ahead, do not add tomatoes until following day.)

Combine dressing ingredients and mix well with salad. Marinate at least 8 hours. It's very attractive served on romaine lettuce leaves with tomato and lemon wedges.

Curried Rice Salad

Serves: 8 to 10
Prepare: 10 min.
Cook: 20 min.
Marinate: overnight

Not only is this delicious, but it's versatile. After cooking rice and adding seasonings and lemon juice, you may serve it hot with fish or lamb. Refrigerate the left-over amount. The next day, proceed as you would with the regular recipe, but adjust remaining ingredients in proportion to quantity of rice.

2 cups long-grain rice
4 cups chicken broth
1 1-inch slice of fresh ginger (or ¼ teaspoon powdered)
1 teaspoon curry powder

½ teaspoon turmeric
½ teaspoon salt
Freshly ground pepper to taste
¼ cup olive oil
Juice of 2 small lemons

Cook rice in broth with ginger, curry, turmeric, salt, and pepper, simmering for 20 minutes or according to package directions. Remove ginger slice and toss rice with olive oil and lemon juice. Refrigerate overnight.

½ cup white raisins
½ cup currants
1 cup chopped green pepper
½ cup mayonnaise

½ cup yogurt
½ cup finely chopped parsley
¼ cup toasted sliced almonds

In the morning, toss the rice with raisins, currants, green pepper, mayonnaise, and yogurt. Taste for seasoning. You may wish to add more lemon and pepper. Refrigerate until serving time.

To serve, sprinkle with parsley and almonds. It makes a nice summer luncheon with *Banana Bread* or *Zucchini Bread* and a watercress salad.

Danish Potato Salad

Serves: 6
Prepare: 20 min.
Chill: 3 hours

This is a good one!

2 tablespoons salad oil
1 clove garlic, split
4–5 medium red-skinned
   potatoes (to make 4 cups)
¼ cup tarragon wine
   vinegar
1 teaspoon salt
1 teaspoon sugar

½ teaspoon dried dill weed
3 hard-cooked eggs
⅓ cup real mayonnaise
1 bunch green onions,
   sliced
3 large radishes, sliced
Chopped parsley

Combine oil and garlic in a jar and let stand. Leaving the pretty skins on, cut potatoes into ½ to ¾-inch cubes. Boil in salted water until just tender. Drain.

Remove garlic from oil, then add vinegar, salt, sugar, and dill weed. Pour over warm potatoes. Cover and refrigerate for several hours.

Near serving time, chop 2 of the 3 eggs and add to potatoes with mayonnaise, onions, and radishes. Slice remaining egg for decorating top of salad, sprinkling chopped parsley over all.

Bean Sprout Salad

Serves: 8 to 12
Prepare: 15 min.
Marinate: 30 min.

A nicely different kind of picnic fare, you can make it two or so hours ahead, but don't add the bacon until serving time.

8 slices bacon, diced
⅓ cup bacon drippings
⅓ cup red wine vinegar
1 clove garlic, minced
½ teaspoon Worcestershire
   sauce

⅛ teaspoon dry mustard
¾ teaspoon salt
Freshly ground pepper
   to taste

Sauté bacon until crisp. Drain on paper towels, reserving ⅓ cup bacon fat. Combine fat with remaining ingredients and heat.

1 pound (1½ quarts) fresh
   bean sprouts (do not
   use canned)
2 bunches green onions,
   chopped

In a colander, wash bean sprouts under *hot* water for 2–3 minutes, to wilt slightly. Drain. Place in bowl with green onions and hot dressing, and marinate at least 30 minutes at room temperature. Add bacon pieces just before serving.

Laredo Salad

Serves: 8 to 10
Prepare: 20 min.

The mint adds something nice to this pretty picnic salad. The real surprise is in the "left-over".

6 tomatoes, cut in small wedges
2 green peppers, cut in thin strips
1 bunch radishes, sliced
1 bunch green onions, chopped

2 avocados, cut in small chunks
1 cucumber, coarsely chopped
½ bunch parsley, chopped
1 tablespoon chopped mint leaves

Dressing

⅓ cup olive oil
½ cup lemon juice (about 3 lemons)

1 teaspoon garlic powder
Salt and pepper to taste

Toss vegetables with dressing and refrigerate until serving, which should be within an hour or two.

If you have any salad left-over, puree it in a blender the next day. Add enough tomato juice to make it the right color and consistency, and serve as a very tasty Gazpacho. Garnish with dollops of sour cream or yogurt.

Asparagus Salad

Serves: 8
Prepare: 20 min.

In this case, we recommend that you not substitute fresh for canned asparagus . . .it's the latter, combined with the dressing's flavors, that makes this so good.

1 large head romaine
   lettuce
1 small head iceberg or
   Bibb lettuce
½ red onion, thinly sliced
2–3 tomatoes, cut in
   small wedges

1 14½-ounce can
   asparagus cuts, drained
4 hard-cooked eggs, sliced
4 ounces Danish blue
   cheese, crumbled

Arrange coarsely torn lettuce leaves in an 18-inch, shallow bowl or sided-platter. Decorate with remaining ingredients in order given.

1¼ cups real mayonnaise
⅓ cup salad oil
1 tablespoon plus 2
   teaspoons French's
   mustard

1 tablespoon white vinegar
1 tablespoon honey

Combine above ingredients and pour over salad. Very pretty on a buffet . . .completes a steak dinner.

Spinach Salad with Radishes

Serves: 6 to 8
Prepare: 10 min.

A very pretty and different touch to the ever-popular spinach salad. You'll like the dressing with almost any combination of greens.

2 bunches spinach
  (1–1¼ pounds)
1 bunch radishes
⅓ cup olive oil
¾-inch squeeze of
  anchovy paste

1 teaspoon Dijon mustard
1. clove garlic, minced
Juice of 1 lime or ½ lemon
Freshly ground pepper

Wash and trim spinach. Slice radishes. Combine remaining ingredients. Toss all just before serving.

Greek Salad

Serves: 8
Prepare: 10 min.

For all of you who are tired of lettuce!

4 large tomatoes, cut
  in wedges
1 English cucumber,
  unpeeled but sliced*
1 green pepper, sliced
½ cup Greek olives*
½ cup crumbled feta
  cheese

3 tablespoons olive oil
½–1 teaspoon oregano
½ teaspoon salt
Freshly ground pepper
  to taste

Combine and serve. *The English cucumber may be replaced with 2 regular cucumbers, peeled. If you can't readily find the salty, dried black olives of Greece, substitute this country's ripe olives, pitted.

Butter Lettuce and Egg Salad

Serves: 4
Prepare: 10 min.

If you're in a rut with tossed green salads, this is a delectable diversion.

- 1 large or 2 small heads
  butter lettuce
- 3 hard-cooked eggs, sliced
- 1 bunch green onions,
  finely chopped
- 6 tablespoons heavy cream
- 2 tablespoons white wine
  or tarragon vinegar
- ¼ teaspoon dry mustard
- 2–3 teaspoons sugar
- ½ teaspoon salt
- ⅛ teaspoon white pepper

Place washed and dried lettuce leaves in salad bowl with sliced eggs and chopped green onions. Just before serving, combine remaining ingredients with a whisk, adjusting sugar according to tartness of vinegar. Whip dressing until quite foamy and pour over greens.

Royal Maile Salad

Serves: 4 to 6
Prepare: 15 min.

The dressing is an excellent blend of flavors. Serve this as a luncheon salad for four, or with a cheese soufflé to serve six.

Juice of ½ lemon
6 ounces baby shrimp
2 avocados, peeled and
   sliced
2 heads butter lettuce

Squeeze lemon juice over shrimp and avocados. Tear lettuce into bite-size pieces. Combine following ingredients, blending oil in slowly.

¼ cup cider vinegar
1 teaspoon Dijon mustard
1 teaspoon celery seeds
½ teaspoon Worcestershire
   sauce
¼ teaspoon garlic salt
   or powder

1 egg, boiled 1 minute
¾ cup salad oil
½–1 teaspoon salt
¼ teaspoon freshly ground
   pepper

Using salad dressing discriminately, toss with shrimp, avocados, and lettuce. Garnish plates with watercress and lemon wedges.

Oriental Chicken Salad

Serves: 6
Prepare: 20 min.

An unusual main-dish salad that's perfect for boating.

1 head cabbage (about 2 pounds)
3–4 cups shredded chicken (about 3 whole breasts)
4 green onions, thinly sliced
⅓ cup chopped toasted almonds

3 tablespoons toasted sesame seeds
1 3-ounce package instant ramen noodles (may use from an oriental soup mix)

Combine all in a large bowl. Prepare the following.

⅓ cup salad oil
¼ cup rice vinegar*
2 tablespoons sugar

1 teaspoon salt
½ teaspoon pepper

Combine and stir until sugar dissolves. *If using "seasoned gourmet" rice vinegar, you may wish to use less sugar.

Do not dress salad until just before serving, so that noodles and nuts stay crisp.

Note: On long boat trips, you can get away with canned chicken. The other flavors and textures hide it.

Fish, Fowl,
and Meats

Crayfish à la Pike Place Market

Serves: 4 to 8
Prepare: 10 min.
Cook: 5–6 min.

Is there any time of the year that THE Market is more in its glory than mid-July through September? This is when you'll find these marvelous, succulent delicacies. Either prepare them as suggested and serve warm with pots of melted butter, bibbs and huge napkins, fingerbowls, and a casserole of Eggplant and Rice Provencal, *or chill and display as a spectacular appetizer.*

60 crayfish
6 quarts boiling water
½ cup salt
Fresh stalks of dill with heads

Wash crayfish thoroughly in cold water. It is vital that they be alive until cooking, so discard any questionables.

To boiling water, add salt and 1 stalk of dill with heads. Boil 2–3 minutes, remove dill, then drop in crayfish. (If heat isn't sufficient, you may have to boil in several batches.) Cover and cook 5 minutes. If serving warm, use a skimmer to remove to serving platter, and decorate with heads of dill. If serving cold, return to pot liquor after it has cooled some, adding another stalk of dill. Steep in refrigerator several hours or overnight. Arrange on a handsome platter with dill heads and small forks.

In Scandinavian-fashion, serve this at an outdoor supper with a bit of Aquavit . . ."One schnapps for every claw!"

Baked Halibut in Light Sour Cream

Serves: 6
Prepare: 5 min.
Marinate: 30 min. plus
Bake: 15 min.

We guarantee that the children will eat fish prepared this way! Marinating in lime juice for a minimum of 30 minutes helps to remove any "fishiness".

2–2½ pounds halibut steaks, cut 1½-inches thick
Juice of 2–3 limes
¼ cup dry white wine
½ cup chopped green onions

1 cup light sour cream
¼ teaspoon white pepper
½ teaspoon salt
Dash of dill weed (optional)
⅓ cup Parmesan Cheese

In a well-buttered, shallow, glass baking dish, marinate halibut in lime juice up to 2 hours, turning periodically.

Preheat oven to 450°. Pour off lime juice and replace with white wine. Bake, uncovered, for 5 minutes.

Combine remaining ingredients. Baste fish with wine then pour sour cream mixture over top. Bake another 10 minutes or until fish begins to flake. Do not overbake.

A good serving suggestion is buttered brown rice and *Sauteed Leeks with Tomatoes*.

Halibut in Orange Sauce

Serves: 6
Prepare: 10 min.
Bake: 20–25 min.

A delicate dish that would suit almost any kind of fish.

2 pounds halibut steaks
½ cup chopped onion
2 cloves garlic, minced
1 tablespoon butter
1 tablespoon oil
2 tablespoons snipped cilantro*

1 teaspoon salt
⅛ teaspoon white pepper
½ cup orange juice
1 tablespoon lemon juice
Orange slices

Preheat oven to 400°. Arrange fish steaks in an ungreased, shallow, 8×12-inch baking dish.

In a small skillet, gently sauté onion and garlic in butter and oil until tender. Stir in cilantro, salt and pepper. Spread mixture over fish. Combine fruit juices and pour over all.

Bake, covered, at 400° for 20–25 minutes, until fish flakes easily with a fork. Do not overbake.

To serve, sprinkle with paprika and garnish with orange slices. Because this dish is so nicely understated, buttered rice and a spinach salad would complete the meal. Oh, yes! *Pears In Raspberry Sauce* for dessert.

*Note: Cilantro is the leaf of the coriander and is also known as Chinese parsley. Regular parsley may be substituted.

Salmon Indian-style

Serves: 6
Prepare: 10 min.
Broil: 20–25 min.

Some Indians may not agree, but this is a tasty facsimile when the weather precludes barbecuing.

5–6 pounds filleted salmon
Garlic powder
Hickory-smoked salt
Brown sugar

Butter
Dried dill weed
1 bunch parsley

Place fish, skin-side down, on piece of foil with crimped edges. With a sharp knife, score the flesh in direction of the grain, ½-inch deep in 1-inch intervals. Lightly dust with garlic powder, hickory-smoked salt, and brown sugar, then rub in with fingers. Dot with butter.

Place on rack in lowest position of oven. Broil with oven door open slightly. After 15 minutes, dust entire fillet with dried dill weed. Continue broiling until flesh begins to slightly brown; about 10 minutes. If fish has not begun to flake, turn off oven and close door for a few minutes, but do not overcook.

Serve with lots of parsley tucked under edges, hot sourdough bread, and your favorite salad or *Eggplant and Rice Provencal*.

Stuffed Salmon

Serves: 6
Prepare: 15 min.
Bake: 30 min.

"I remember my mother serving this on very special, warm, summer evenings, out-of-doors." (A food processor will make the preparation a breeze.)

1 4-pound salmon, cleaned
2 tablespoons chopped onions
2 tablespoons chopped mushrooms
2 tablespoons chopped ripe olives
1 tablespoon finely chopped green pepper
1 tablespoon finely chopped parsley
¼ teaspoon basil
½ teaspoon salt
Freshly ground pepper to taste
1 cup fine, fresh bread crumbs (whole wheat or 7-grain)
¼ cup butter, melted
4 bacon strips

Wash and dry salmon. Combine remaining ingredients, except bacon, and stuff salmon.

Top salmon with bacon strips and place on sheet of heavy-duty foil on top of barbecue grill. Bake (lid down) as you would in oven: at 400° for 20–30 minutes, 350° for 30–40 minutes, or at 300° for 40 minutes.

"She served it with lemon wedges, baked potatoes, just-picked corn-on-the-cob, hot sourdough bread, and fresh spinach salad."

Audrey's Fish Stew

Serves: 6 to 8
Prepare: 20 min.
Cook: 30 min.
10 min.

Simply delicious. Serve in large bowls and pass buttered, sourdough bread for heavenly dipping.

1 large onion, chopped
½ cup chopped celery
   with leaves
1 large clove garlic, minced
2 tablespoons butter
2 16-ounce cans tomatoes,
   cut up
½ cup dry white wine

½ cup chopped parsley
¼ teaspoon thyme
1 teaspoon salt
¼ teaspoon pepper
1 salmon bone*
1 7-ounce can salmon,
   drained

In 6-quart kettle, sauté onion, celery, and garlic in butter until tender. Stir in remaining ingredients except canned salmon. Cover and simmer 30 minutes.

Remove salmon bone, leaving any meat in soup base. Add canned salmon. Soup may be set aside until 10 minutes or so before serving time.

2 dozen steamer clams,
   scrubbed
2½ pounds firm white fish,
   cut in chunks*
1 pound raw shrimp,
   shelled and deveined

1–2 Dungeness crabs,
   cooked, cleaned,
   and cracked

For final preparation, reheat soup. Add clams and simmer 3 minutes. Add fish and shrimp. Simmer 3 more minutes or until fish is translucent, clams have opened, and shrimp are pink. Add crab just to heat through.

Serve immediately in warmed bowls with big napkins and bibs on hand, and a chilled bottle of crisp white wine.

Note: Your fishmonger will provide you with the backbone of a filleted salmon. Audrey suggests using cod as the white fish. The markets sell it as "fish and chips chunks".

Grilled Chicken Breasts in Red Wine

Serves: 6 to 8
Prepare: 5–10 min.
Marinate: 2–3 hours
Barbecue: 6 min.

A wonderful "company dish" with little effort.

4 whole chicken breasts, boned, skinned, and split
1 cup red wine
½ cup oil
¼ cup soy sauce

2 teaspoons powdered ginger
1 teaspoon crushed oregano

Marinate chicken breasts in remaining ingredients for 2–3 hours. Charcoal-broil for 3 minutes on each side. Delicious served with baked potatoes and *Zucchini and Mushrooms*.

Lemony Barbecued Chicken

Serves: 6
Prepare: 5 min.
Marinate: 2–3 hours
Barbecue: 20–30 min.

A light, low-calorie marinade that will surprise and delight you as it did its testers, who were prepared for just another teriyaki-type recipe.

6 chicken breasts, split*
½ cup lemon juice (2 large lemons)
¼ cup water
3 tablespoons soy sauce

¼ teaspoon powdered ginger
1 teaspoon garlic powder (or 1 clove, crushed)

*Any part of the chicken will be good in this marinade, but wing joints are superb! Combine remaining ingredients and marinate chicken in refrigerator, covered, for 2–3 hours.

Barbecue on outdoor grill or hibachi, or under your broiler, basting frequently with marinade, until tender.

Good with rice dishes or *Potatoes Dauphinoise*, grilled corn-on-the-cob, and a green leaf salad.

Eddy's Chicken Kiev

Serves: 4 to 6
Prepare: 30 min.
Bake: 45 min.

An easier, different approach to this ever-popular entree ... so good that it starred in the menu for "Dinner for Ten", an Overlake School Auction item.

4 whole chicken breasts,
  boned and skinned
½ pound butter
½ cup chopped parsley
½ cup chopped green
  onion

4 ounces Monterey
  jack cheese
8 thin slices ham
2 eggs, beaten
1½ cups fine bread
  crumbs*

*Bread that is several days old, spun into crumbs in your food processor, gives an ideal texture.

Preheat oven to 350°. Cut chicken breasts in half and place between two sheets of wax paper. Pound with a mallet until uniformly ¼-inch thick.

Melt butter over low heat, adding parsley and green onions.

Cut cheese into 3 × ½-inch "sticks". With breasts smooth-side down, top each with a ham slice and piece of cheese. Roll up, tucking in ends, and secure with toothpicks.

Dip breasts in beaten eggs and roll in crumbs. Place, seam-side down, in ungreased, shallow 8 × 12-inch casserole. Pour butter mixture over all. Bake, uncovered, at 350° for 45 minutes, basting several times.

Serve with *Pete White's Savory Rice* and broccoli or asparagus with *Hollandaise Sauce*, then top everything off with *Pots de Crème* for dessert.

Chicken Breasts Florentine

Serves: 4 to 6
Prepare: 30 min.
Bake: 20–25 min.

Fresh spinach adds much to the subtle blending of the good flavors in this recipe. Everyone loved this menu.

3 large, whole chicken
   breasts, halved
1 celery stalk, cut in
   several pieces

1 small onion, quartered
Sprig or 2 of parsley
1 teaspoon vinegar
½ teaspoon salt

Place all of above in a large frying pan with just enough water to cover. Cover and simmer until just tender; about 15–20 minutes. Strain broth, reserving 1 cup. Discard vegetables. Bone and skin chicken.

3 pounds fresh spinach
¼ cup butter
¼ cup flour
½ teaspoon salt
Dash of white pepper

1 cup reserved broth
1 cup light cream
½ cup grated Parmesan
   cheese
Grating of nutmeg

Preheat oven to 375°. Wash spinach and place in pot with only water that clings to leaves. Cover and cook until just tender; about 2–3 minutes. Drain well, squeezing out excess moisture. Chop.

Melt butter in a saucepan. With a whisk, blend in flour, salt and pepper. Slowly stir in reserved broth and cream. Cook, stirring, until thickened and bubbly.

Stir half of sauce into drained spinach, along with half of Parmesan cheese, plus the nutmeg. Spread spinach mixture in lightly buttered, shallow, 6×10-inch baking dish. Arrange chicken breasts on top. Pour remaining sauce over all, and sprinkle with rest of cheese and another light sprinkling of nutmeg. Bake, uncovered, until lightly browned; about 20–25 minutes.

Through the sheer necessity of testing, a delicious menu was created that normally would not have been chosen, due to spicy contrasts. Try this dish with *Brown Rice Pilaf* and *Greek Salad*.

Chicken Breasts Jarlsberg

Serves: 6 to 8
Prepare: 10 min.
Bake: 35–50 min.

With no effort, you can have a superb dinner for family or company. The Jarlsberg cheese gives great flavor.

4 whole chicken breasts, split, skinned, and boned
⅓ pound Jarlsberg cheese, sliced
1 medium zucchini, thinly sliced
1 can cream of mushroom soup

¼ cup dry white wine
Salt and pepper (optional)
Garlic powder (optional)
1 8-ounce package (2 cups) Pepperidge Farm herbed stuffing mix (not the cubes)
⅓ cup melted butter

Preheat oven to 350°. Butter a shallow, 9×13-inch baking dish. Arrange chicken breasts in bottom. Top breasts with cheese slices. Cover with thin zucchini slices.

Combine soup and wine and pour over zucchini. If you wish, lightly season with salt, pepper, and garlic powder. Sprinkle stuffing mix over all. Drizzle with melted butter.

Bake, uncovered, at 350° for 35–50 minutes, until chicken is cooked through and casserole is bubbly.

Chicken Parmigiana

Serves: 4 to 6
Prepare: 25 min.
Bake: 35 min.

Delicious, easy, attractive, popular . . .what more can we say?

3 whole chicken breasts, boned
2 eggs, slightly beaten
1 teaspoon salt
Freshly ground pepper
¾ cup fine bread crumbs
½ cup vegetable oil
2 cups tomato sauce
¼ teaspoon basil
⅛ teaspoon garlic powder
8 ounces mozzarella cheese, sliced
½ cup grated Parmesan cheese

Preheat oven to 350°. Skin, split, and bone chicken breasts. (If you have the time, freeze breasts 15 minutes for easier boning.) Combine eggs, salt and pepper. Dip breasts in egg mixture, then bread crumbs, coating both sides.

In large skillet, heat oil to very hot. Brown chicken quickly on both sides. Drain and remove to shallow, 9×13-inch baking dish. Discard excess oil. In same pan, simmer tomato sauce, basil, and garlic powder for 10 minutes, or until thickened.

Place a slice of mozzarella cheese on top of each browned chicken breast. Pour tomato sauce over chicken and cheese. Sprinkle Parmesan cheese over all and bake, uncovered, for 30–35 minutes, until light, golden brown and bubbly.

Note: Slices of turkey breast may be prepared this way.

Sweet and Sour Chicken

Serves: 8
Prepare: 5 min.
Bake: 1¼ hours

It sounds simply awful, but it's really simply delicious.

4 whole chicken breasts, split
4 whole chicken legs
1 18-ounce jar apricot preserves

1 8-ounce bottle Russian dressing
1 envelope onion soup mix

Preheat oven to 350°. Place chicken pieces in a large, shallow baking dish. Combine remaining ingredients and pour over to coat all of chicken. Bake, uncovered, 1¼ hours. Brown rice is just right with this.

Chicken Indonesia

Serves: 6
Prepare: 10 min.
Marinate: 2–3 hours
Bake: 45 min.

Once you discover this recipe, you'll be addicted. The marinating is not an absolute must, but it will make it just that much better.

3 broilers, split in half or quarters
2 tablespoons curry powder

½ cup French's mustard
½ cup honey
2 tablespoons soy sauce

Rinse and dry chicken thoroughly. Combine remaining ingredients and rub over all of chicken. Cover and let stand in refrigerator for several hours or overnight.

Preheat oven to 375°. Spread chicken on foil-lined cookie sheets and bake 45–60 minutes, until tender and golden brown. Baste every 15 minutes with any leftover sauce.

As a serving suggestion, try *Brown Rice Pilaf* and steamed broccoli or asparagus with *Hollandaise Sauce*.

Baked Chicken in Lemon

Serves: 4
Prepare: 25 min.
Bake: 40 min.

A very good version that's especially nice as a "left-over" for picnic fare.

1 2½-pound chicken, quartered
¼ cup butter
2 tablespoons salad oil
2 tablespoons chopped onion

1 clove garlic, crushed
1 teaspoon thyme
½ teaspoon salt
½ cup lemon juice (or more, if you love lemon)

Wash and dry chicken. Season with a sprinkling of salt and freshly ground pepper. Melt butter in skillet and slowly brown pieces, turning with tongs. When well-browned, place in a shallow baking dish.

Combine remaining ingredients and add to pan drippings. Over moderate heat, deglaze, then pour over chicken.

Bake, uncovered, at 325° for 30–40 minutes, basting periodically. Pour sauce over chicken when serving.

Gingered Carrots and a bright green vegetable give the right flavor and color accents.

Chicken Chile Casserole

Serves: 6 to 8
Prepare: 25 min.
Cook: 25 min.
Bake: 45 min.

Appeals to all ages.

4 whole chicken breasts
½ cup water
1 cup chicken broth
1 cup milk
1 can cream of mushroom soup
1 tablespoon grated onion
1 4-ounce can diced green chilies

9 corn tortillas, cut in 1-inch pieces
1 cup sliced ripe olives (optional)
1 pound cheddar cheese, shredded

Place chicken in skillet with ½ cup water. Tightly cover and simmer until tender, about 20–25 minutes. Reserve broth, adding enough water to make 1 cup. Shred chicken into bite-size pieces.

Combine broth, milk, mushroom soup, onion, and chilies. Stir in chicken. Layer bottom of a buttered, 9×13-inch, shallow baking dish with half of tortilla pieces. Layer half of chicken mixture, half of olives, and half of cheese. Repeat.

Bake, uncovered, at 350° for 45 minutes, or covered, at 400° for 30 minutes. Casserole should be bubbly and heated through. Serve with a salad of sliced tomatoes and avocados, drizzled with lime juice.

Chinese Chicken Wings

Serves: 4 to 6
Prepare: 30 min.
Bake: 45–55 min.

Once we started testing these, the butcher couldn't keep enough on hand! Kids love them.

2½-3 pounds chicken wings
Garlic salt
¾ cup sugar
½ cup pineapple juice
½ cup vinegar
¼ cup catsup

1 teaspoon soy sauce
½ teaspoon salt (optional)
1 or 2 eggs, beaten
1 cup flour
Oil

If chicken wings were packaged untrimmed, remove wing tips and discard. Sprinkle lightly with garlic salt and let stand while preparing sauce.

Preheat oven to 350°. In a 1-quart saucepan, combine sugar, pineapple juice, vinegar, catsup, soy sauce, and salt. Heat to dissolve sugar, then pour over chicken.

Dip chicken in beaten egg, then flour. Heat oil in skillet over medium-high heat. Fry wings until brown, turning with tongs. Place in ungreased, shallow, 3-quart baking dish.

Pour sauce over chicken and bake, covered, for 25 minutes. Turn chicken pieces over, coating each with sauce. Replace cover and bake an additional 20–25 minutes.

Serve with rice (the extra sauce is delicious spooned over it), and *Spinach Salad with Radishes.*

Chicken Liver Scramble

Serves: 4
Prepare: 20 min.

Bacon and wine do wonderful things for chicken livers.

6 slices bacon, diced
1 pound chicken livers, cleaned
Flour
1 medium onion, chopped

6 ounces fresh mushrooms, sliced
½ cup dry white wine
Salt and pepper to taste

In large, heavy skillet, sauté bacon until crisp. Drain on paper toweling, reserving 2–3 tablespoons of fat in skillet.

Cut livers into bite-size pieces and lightly flour. Over medium high heat, brown quickly in bacon fat and set aside. Reduce heat to moderate. Sauté onion and mushrooms until soft, adding more fat only if necessary.

Return livers and bacon to skillet and add wine. Cover and simmer over medium-low heat for 3–5 minutes. Serve over rice.

Rock Cornish Game Hens with Fresh Herbs

Serves: 4 to 6
Prepare: 10 min.
Marinate: 2–3 hours
Bake: 50–60 min.

Marvelous, subtle flavors, and the hens stay moist and tender.

3 game hens
¼ cup olive oil
Juice of 2–3 limes
2 tablespoons minced
   sage leaves
2 tablespoons chopped
   mint leaves

2 cloves garlic, minced
1 teaspoon salt
½ teaspoon freshly
   ground pepper
3 drops Tabasco

Split hens in half. Wash and dry well with paper towels. Place in shallow, 9×13-inch baking dish.

Combine remaining ingredients and pour over hens. Cover and refrigerate 2–3 hours, turning hens in marinade several times.

Preheat oven to 450°. Roast, uncovered, 20 minutes. Lower temperature to 400°. Bake 30–40 more minutes until hens are golden brown and tender, basting every 10–15 minutes.

Skagit Valley Wild Duck

Serves: 6
Prepare: 30 min.
Marinate: 6–8 hours
Broil: 10 min.

We defy you to find an easier, better recipe for duck! It's basically an entree, but try it as an h'ors d'oeuvre with Mustard Sauce *and* crackers.

6 whole duck breasts
¼ cup soy sauce
3 tablespoons olive oil
3 tablespoons dry sherry
½ teaspoon grated ginger
2 cloves garlic, minced

Bone duck breasts into 12 fillets. Combine remaining ingredients and pour over duck in glass bowl. Turn to baste. Cover and refrigerate 6–8 hours.

Be sure that duck breasts reach room temperature before preparing. Either barbecue over hot coals or broil 3–4 inches from heat; approximately 4–5 minutes per side. Baste once or twice with reserved marinade. Duck should still be pink in middle.

Slice very thin and serve with *Lida's Wild Rice*, a crisp green salad, French bread, and a good red wine.

Scotch Eggs

Serves: 4 to 6
Prepare: 20 min.
Bake: 25 min.

Just reading this recipe will not reveal how wonderful the dish is. At least it was a big sur-prise to its testers. Ideal for brunch or special suppers.

8 hard-cooked eggs
1 pound pork sausage
½–¾ cup fine bread
    crumbs
¼ teaspoon paprika
1 egg, beaten

Preheat oven to 375°. After cooking the eggs, be sure that they are immediately immersed in ice-cold water until chilled through. This will prevent any darkening of the yolks.

On lightly floured surface, flatten sausage to 8×8-inch square. Cut into 8 sections. Mold a piece around each egg, completely covering it.

Combine breadcrumbs and paprika. Dip covered eggs into beaten egg, then into crumbs. Place in ungreased, shallow baking dish. Bake at 375° for 20–25 minutes, until lightly browned.

A delicious menu suggestion is to serve these surrounded by lightly creamed fresh spinach that's had a grating of nutmeg. Mound *Gingered Carrots* at each end of the platter and pass a sauceboat of *Mustard Cream*.

Deepdish Zucchini Pizza

Serves: 4 to 6
Prepare: 25 min.
Bake: 30 min.

The incredibly versatile zucchini serves as the crust for this really good creation. Omit the sausage for a vegetarian entree.

4 cups shredded zucchini, well-squeezed
¾ cup shredded Monterey jack cheese
¾ cup shredded sharp cheddar cheese
2 eggs, lightly beaten

Preheat oven to 400°. Zucchini must be squeezed of all excess moisture. Combine with cheeses and lightly beaten eggs. Press into a buttered, shallow 9½ × 13½-inch roasting pan (a glass baking dish would not be deep enough).

¾–1 pound bulk sausage (or thinly sliced hot dogs)
1 medium onion, chopped
2 cloves garlic, minced
1 6-ounce can tomato paste
½ can water
2 tablespoons chopped oregano leaves (2 teaspoons dried)
2 tablespoons chopped basil leaves (2 teaspoons dried)

In skillet, lightly brown sausage or hot dog slices, using no fat, if possible. Add onion and garlic, cooking until soft. Pour off any fat. Stir in tomato paste and water, then herbs. Simmer for a minute or so, then spoon over zucchini.

1 green pepper, seeded and cut in thin strips
¼ pound mushrooms, sliced
½ cup grated Parmesan cheese
¾ cup shredded Monterey jack cheese
¾ cup shredded sharp cheddar cheese

Arrange green pepper strips and mushroom slices on top. Sprinkle with cheeses. Bake, uncovered, at 400° for 30 minutes, until cheeses are bubbly.

Pork Chops in Orange Sauce

Serves: 6
Prepare: 15 min.
Cook: 1–1½ hours

An easy way to make a family dinner glamorous for spur-of-the-moment company.

6 fairly thick pork steaks
   or chops
2 teaspoons dry mustard
1 teaspoon salt
¼ teaspoon freshly
   ground pepper
1 tablespoon butter
2–3 cloves garlic, crushed

½ cup dry vermouth
½ cup dry white wine
1 cup orange juice
2 tablespoons flour
3 tablespoons water
Orange slices
Parsley

Rub pork with mixture of dry mustard, salt and pepper. In a heavy skillet, melt butter with garlic, and brown chops. Add liquids and simmer, covered, over low heat for 1–1½ hours, until chops are tender.

Remove chops to a warm platter. Make paste of flour and water, and add to pan liquids over medium heat, stirring with a flat whisk until gravy is smooth and desired consistency.

To serve, pour some of gravy over pork chops, garnishing with orange slices and parsley. Pass remaining gravy in a sauce boat. Excellent with short grain brown rice, *Gingered Carrots*, and *Sassy Zucchini*.

Stuffed Pork Chops

Serves: 6
Prepare: 25 min.
Cook: 1–½ hours

. . .somehow suits autumn. Add Fried Apples for a delicious garnish.

6 pork chops, 1½ to 1¾-inches thick
2 cups Pepperidge Farm seasoned bread cubes
½ cup finely chopped celery
½ cup finely chopped onion
2 tablespoons finely chopped parsley
½ teaspoon poultry seasoning
½ teaspoon salt
¼ teaspoon freshly ground pepper
2 tablespoons melted butter
¼ cup hot water

Have butcher cut pockets into chops for stuffing. Combine remaining ingredients and toss. Lightly stuff chops and fasten openings with toothpicks, lacing with string.

In large skillet, brown chops over medium-high heat, searing fat edges first to grease pan. Reduce heat, add ½ cup hot water, and cover tightly. Simmer 1–1½ hours or until tender.

Pork Picadillo

Serves: 8
Prepare: 35 min.
Cook: 45 min.

This is an ideal recipe for casual entertaining, and fun to present. The long list of ingredients just means that it's good! It is very easy to prepare.

3½ pounds boneless pork shoulder
1 large onion, chopped
2 tablespoons butter
2 tablespoons oil
2 cloves garlic, minced
2 cups tomato sauce

½ cup chili sauce
2 teaspoons salt
1 teaspoon cinnamon
¼ teaspoon ground cumin
½ cup dried currants
3 tablespoons cider vinegar
3 tablespoons brown sugar

Cut pork into ¾-inch cubes. In a Dutch oven, sauté onion in butter and oil. When soft, use a slotted spoon to transfer to a large bowl. Brown meat in small batches, setting aside with onion. Return meat and onion to pan, along with remaining ingredients. Cover and simmer 45 minutes, or until meat is tender.

16 flour tortillas
1 bunch green onions, slivered
2 avocados, peeled and sliced
Lime juice
3 limes, cut in wedges

To serve, warm tortillas in a foil packet in oven. Garnish Picadillo with green onion, and provide a side dish of avocados drizzled with lime juice and surrounded with lime wedges. Placing the tortillas in a napkin-lined basket, instruct your guests to fill each with the Picadillo and avocado, then a squeeze of lime juice.

If you wish, provide a pot of refried beans or a platter of steaming corn-on-the-cob, and green salad.

Chili Con Carne

Serves: 6
Prepare: 45 min.
Cook: 2 hours

Don't pass by this one. It beats them all!
Fabulous the next day.

6 slices bacon, cut into 1-inch pieces
2 cups chopped onions
4 cloves garlic, chopped
3 pounds lean pork shoulder, cut in ½-inch cubes
¼ to ⅓ cup chili powder
2 16-ounce cans tomatoes in purée
1 cup beer
1 4-ounce can chopped green chilies

2 jalapeño chilies, seeded and finely chopped
1 teaspoon oregano
1 bay leaf
2 to 3 dried red chilies (Japanese chilies, if you really like it hot)
2 16-ounce cans pinto or kidney beans
1 4-ounce can ripe olives, sliced

In a large Dutch oven, brown bacon. Add onions and garlic, sautéing until soft. With a slotted spoon, remove to a colander, returning as much fat as possible to pan by pressing. In same pan and in small batches, brown pork lightly on all sides and drain in colander.

When finished browning, wipe all fat from pan then return meat and onion mixture. Add chili powder and cook for 2 minutes, stirring occasionally. Add tomatoes, beer, chilies, oregano, bay leaf, and red chilies (optional). Simmer, uncovered, for 1 hour, stirring occasionally.

Add beans and olives. Simmer another ¾ to 1 hour (covered, if too thick) until pork is tender and sauce has thickened. Discard bay leaf and red chilies. (The latter will do you in if you eat them!) Skim fat.

Serve as is or with any or all of suggested garnishes and warmed flour tortillas or hunks of French bread.

Garnishes: avocado chunks, grated cheddar cheese, chopped green onions, sour cream, olives . . .whatever you like!

Sherry-glazed Spareribs

Serves: 4 to 6
Prepare: 10 min.
Bake: 2 hours

A really good family dinner.

3½–4 pounds pork spare-
  ribs or "country-style"
1 15-ounce can tomato
  sauce
½ cup cooking sherry
½ cup honey
2 tablespoons red
  wine vinegar

2 tablespoons minced
  onion
1 clove garlic, crushed
1 teaspoon Worcestershire
  sauce
Salt and freshly ground
  pepper to taste

Preheat oven to 400°. Season ribs with salt and pepper and place on rack in shallow roasting pan. Bake, uncovered, for 40 minutes. Drain off all fat.

Combine remaining ingredients and pour over ribs. Reduce oven temperature to 350°. Bake, uncovered, 1 to 1½ hours more, until tender. Baste periodically.

Serve with *Sour Cream Potatoes* or *Savory Rice* and a seasonal green vegetable.

Veal Stew with Sausage

Serves: 6
Prepare: 25 min.
Cook: 2 hours

This flavorful stew is dressy enough for company.

3 pounds breast of veal*
3 tablespoons salad oil
Flour
1 link Italian hot sausage,
   cut in ½-inch thick slices
1 large onion, chopped
½ pound fresh mushrooms,
   sliced
1 1½-ounce envelope
   spaghetti sauce with
   mushrooms mix

2 cups hot water
1 8-ounce can tomato sauce
6 carrots, cut in 3-inch
   pieces
3 medium zucchini, sliced
   ¼-inch thick

* This cut of veal can be ordered from the butcher as "veal fricassee". There is a lot of bone in it, but that is what makes the dish so flavorful. Ask your butcher to run it through his saw for stew-size pieces.

Heat oil in a large kettle or Dutch oven. Dust veal with flour and brown quickly in small batches, using a slotted spoon to set aside. In same kettle, partially brown sausage, then add onion and mushrooms. Sauté until onion is translucent. Return veal to pan. Stir in spaghetti sauce mix, hot water, and tomato sauce. Bring to a boil and simmer, covered, one hour.

Add cut carrots to veal and simmer another 45 minutes, or until tender. Add sliced zucchini, and simmer 15 minutes. Check seasoning.

This can become a special autumn dinner when served with buttered noodles, a salad of watercress garnished with walnuts, and *Frozen Pumpkin Pie* for dessert.

Lamb Stew with Spring Vegetables

Serves: 6
Prepare: 30–40 min.
Bake: 30 min.
     50 min.

Lean shoulder of lamb is a good choice for this savory stew. Leaving the bone in adds much flavor.

3½ pounds lamb shoulder,
    bone in
Flour
3 tablespoons oil
2 cups chicken broth
1 clove garlic, minced

Preheat oven to 350°. Cut lamb into stew-size pieces and lightly flour. Sauté in hot oil until browned, removing to a 4-quart casserole. Add broth and garlic to casserole. Cover and bake 30 minutes. Drain any grease from frying pan but do not clean.

12 small, red-skinned
    potatoes, unpeeled
 · 3 tablespoons butter
4–5 carrots, cut in 1-inch
    slices
3 parsnips or turnips,
    cut up

2 medium onions, sliced
1½ tablespoons sugar
1–1½ cups fresh peas
    (or 1 box frozen)
Salt and pepper to taste

Parboil potatoes until barely tender. Drain. In same frying pan, melt 3 tablespoons butter and sauté carrots, turnips, and onions for 5 minutes. Sprinkle with sugar and cook, stirring, 5 more minutes, or until well-glazed.

After meat has cooked 30 minutes, add glazed vegetables and potatoes. Continue baking, covered, 50 more minutes or until meat and vegetables are tender. Add peas during last 5–10 minutes. Season with salt and pepper, if necessary.

You'll need little else with this but hot, crusty bread or biscuits, a bottle of rosé or riesling, and *Angel Lemon Delight* for dessert!

Speedies

Serves: 2 to 3
Prepare: 5 min.
Marinate: 3 to 6 days

These are so much fun! We're not sure of the spelling, but we do know that the recipe was imported from the southern tip of New York State where these are a local favorite. Might be a great menu item for the hibachi during a summer cruise of the San Juans.

1 pound lamb, cut in
   1-inch cubes
¼ cup vegetable oil
¼ cup red wine vinegar
3 tablespoons lemon juice
1 tablespoon oregano
1 tablespoon dried
   onion flakes

1 garlic clove, split
¼ teaspoon salt
¼ teaspoon freshly
   ground pepper
French rolls

Place lamb and remaining ingredients (except rolls) in a plastic bag and seal tightly. Marinate in refrigerator at least 3 days or up to a week.

Place lamb cubes on skewers and barbecue over charcoal to desired doneness. Serve in French rolls. You won't want anything else with these except a simple green salad and maybe a jug of red wine. Recipe is easily prepared in larger quantities.

Note: If short of skewers, wooden ones can readily be found in the supermarket baking section. Soak in water for several hours before using.

Moussaka

Serves: 12
Prepare: 45 min.
Bake: 1 hour
Cool: 20 min.

*Even in Greece, one seldom finds two mous-
sakas alike, but we defy you to find one better
than this! Make a day ahead or freeze. Just
reheat to serve.*

> 3 medium-sized eggplants
> (about 3 pounds), peeled
> ½ cup olive oil

Preheat oven to 425°. Cut eggplants lengthwise into ½-inch slices.
Divide oil between 2 large baking pans. Quickly coat both sides of
eggplant slices in oil before arranging in single layer in pans. Bake
20 minutes until tender and brown, turning once or twice.

> 3 large onions, chopped
> ¼ cup butter
> 2½ pounds lean ground
> beef or lamb
> 3 tablespoons tomato paste
> ½ cup red wine

> ½ cup chopped parsley
> ¼ teaspoon cinnamon
> 1 teaspoon salt
> ¼ teaspoon freshly
> ground pepper

In large, heavy skillet, sauté onions in butter until soft. Add meat
and cook gently until all pink is gone. Stir remaining ingredients
into meat and simmer until liquid is absorbed; about 5 minutes.
Pour off any fat and set aside while making cream sauce.

> ½ cup butter
> 6 tablespoons flour
> 1 quart milk, heated
> 4 eggs, beaten
> 2 cups small curd
> cottage cheese

> ¼ teaspoon nutmeg
> ¾ teaspoon salt
> 1 cup fine bread crumbs
> 1 cup grated Parmesan
> cheese

Preheat oven to 375°. In large saucepan, melt butter and blend in
flour with a whisk. Add hot milk, stirring until thickened. Cool. Stir in
beaten eggs, cottage cheese, nutmeg, and salt.

Grease an 11×16-inch pan or 18-inch oval casserole. Lightly sprinkle bottom with some of bread crumbs. Arrange alternate layers of eggplant and meat in pan, sprinkling each meat layer with Parmesan cheese and bread crumbs.

Pour cream sauce over top and bake, uncovered, at 375° for 1 hour or until top is golden. Cool 20 minutes before cutting into squares for serving.

Serve with *Greek Salad* and hot, crusty bread . . .maybe a bottle of Greek wine, such as Domestica?

Chello Kebab

Serves: 6 to 8
Prepare: 30 min.
Marinate: 2–3 days
Barbecue: 15 min.

During a last-minute search for an unusual lamb recipe to fit this space, our book designer, Kim Bacon, offered her favorite dish from a three-year sojourn in the Middle East. The serving instructions are intriguing.

1 leg of lamb, boned
2 onions, grated
2 cups yogurt

Cut lamb into ½-inch thick strips, approximately 1×2½ inches. Combine with onions and yogurt. Cover and marinate 2–3 days in refrigerator.

Thirty minutes before serving, prepare enough rice to yield 10–12 cups. Thread lamb strips on sturdy metal skewers. Grill over medium to medium-hot coals, turning frequently; about 15 minutes. Meat should be lightly singed but not burned, and still pink in middle. On a heated platter, spread 2 cups of hot rice (cooked quite dry). Alternate layers of grilled lamb and rice until you have a steaming, white mountain in which the succulent chello kebab is hidden.

Modify this as you wish, but Kim says that in Iran, raw egg yolks, sitting in their half-shells (nested in a bed of flour), are offered. Each diner pours a yolk over his serving, the heat of the food cooking it. To the side, set pickled mangos or a hot-sour chutney, and, if you're lucky enough to find it, powdered sumac to sprinkle over all.

Joe's Special

Serves: 4
Prepare: 10 min.

A transplanted San Franciscan brought this to us. The origin has become hazy over the years, but it supposedly was created by Joe of "Original Joe's" restaurant, there. Every family should have this recipe in its files for a quick, delicious supper.

½ pound fresh spinach (or
   1 10-ounce package
   frozen)
1 onion, chopped
1 clove garlic, minced
1 tablespoon oil
1 tablespoon butter

1 pound lean ground beef
½ teaspoon basil
¼ teaspoon marjoram
1 teaspoon salt
¼ teaspoon freshly
   ground pepper
4–5 eggs, lightly beaten

If using fresh spinach, cook until just tender. Squeeze cooked or thawed spinach until rid of excess moisture. Chop.

Heat oil and butter in a large, heavy skillet. Sauté onion and garlic until soft. Add beef and brown. Sprinkle with basil, marjoram, salt and pepper. Stir in spinach. Keeping heat high, add eggs to skillet, constantly stirring and lifting with a metal spatula until eggs are cooked. It should take only a minute. Serve immediately.

Pita breads that have been split, buttered, and sprinkled with Parmesan cheese, then broiled, are perfect with this.

Korean Broiled Flank Steak

Serves: 4 to 6
Prepare: 10 min.
Marinate: 5–6 hours

The sesame seeds take this out of the norm.

2–3 pounds flank steak
3 tablespoons toasted
  sesame seeds
½ cup soy sauce
¼ cup oil
⅓ cup brown sugar

2 green onions, sliced
2 cloves garlic, crushed
½ teaspoon powdered
  ginger
½ teaspoon freshly ground
  black pepper

Lightly score both sides of flank steaks. Combine remaining ingredients and marinate steaks a minimum of 5 hours, preferably overnight. Turn several times in marinade.

Broil or barbecue 3–6 minutes on each side, depending on fire. Nice with *Baked Potato Wedges* and asparagus with *Hollandaise Sauce*.

Porcupine Meatballs

Serves: 4
Prepare: 25 min.
Cook: 8 min.

Just as the title would indicate, these are popular with children.

1 pound lean ground beef
1 egg, beaten
1 cup raw instant rice
1 teaspoon Italian
  seasoning
½ teaspoon chili powder
1 teaspoon salt
¼ teaspoon pepper
1 large onion, chopped
½ cup tomato sauce
2 tablespoons olive oil
2½ cups tomato sauce
3–4 medium zucchini,
  sliced

Combine ground beef, egg, rice, seasonings, half of the chopped onion, and ½ cup tomato sauce. Gently shape into 1½ to 2-inch meat balls.

Heat oil in a large, heavy skillet. Brown meatballs in several batches, turning carefully with a spatula.

Pour off excess fat. Add remaining 2½ cups tomato sauce, rest of chopped onion, and the sliced zucchini. Cover and simmer until zucchini is tender, about 8 minutes.

If you would like to serve something different from the old, faithful, green salad and crusty bread, try *Carrot and Cauliflower Medley* . . .they are a nice combo.

Company Lasagne

Serves: 8 to 10
Prepare: 45 min.
Bake: 1 hour

Make a day ahead, if you wish. It's great for buffets or boating suppers.

1½ pounds lean ground beef
1 large onion, chopped
2 cloves garlic, minced
1 28-ounce can Italian-style pear tomatoes
1 6-ounce can tomato paste
1 teaspoon basil
1 teaspoon sugar

1 pint sour cream
1 8-ounce package cream cheese
1 pint cottage cheese
12 ounces mozzarella cheese, shredded (or more to taste)
½ pound lasagne noodles, cooked al dente

Preheat oven to 375°. Brown meat, adding onions and garlic. Chop canned tomatoes with juice. Add to meat along with tomato paste, basil, and sugar. Simmer, uncovered, until thickened; from 15 to 30 minutes. Stir occasionally.

Combine sour cream, cream cheese, and cottage cheese. Butter a deep, 9×13-inch lasagne pan, and layer noodles, beef, cheese mixture, and mozzarella. Repeat. Bake, uncovered, for 1 hour.

Burritos

Serves: 4 to 6
Prepare: 20 min.
Cook: 30 min.
Bake: 10 min.

There are burritos, and then there are burritos.
But there are no burritos like these burritos!
A fun supper that stands alone.

2 tablespoons oil
1 medium onion, chopped
½ green pepper, chopped
1–2 cloves garlic, minced
1 pound lean ground beef
1 15½-ounce can
   tomato sauce

1 15-ounce can pinto beans
1 teaspoon chili powder
½ teaspoon ground cumin
   seed (comino)
¼ teaspoon ground
   oregano
Salt to taste

Heat oil in a skillet and sauté onion, green pepper, and garlic until limp. Add meat to brown until pink is gone. Pour off any fat, then add tomato sauce. Simmer 5 minutes before adding pinto beans and seasonings. Simmer, uncovered, 30 minutes.

6–8 flour tortillas
   (as fresh as possible)
2 bunches green onions,
   chopped

½ pound Monterey jack
   cheese, shredded
½ head of lettuce, shredded
Taco sauce

Preheat oven to 350°. Tear 6 pieces of regular-strength, aluminum foil, large enough to wrap a tortilla. Place tortilla on foil. Spoon meat mixture down center. Sprinkle with green onions and a goodly amount of shredded cheese. Roll tortilla up so that seam-side is down, tucking ends under. Pleat foil packet so that it is sealed but can be easily opened, and place on a cookie sheet.

Heat foil-wrapped burritos in oven about 10 minutes. To eat, open foil so that it acts as a shallow bowl. Top with a handful of shredded lettuce and taco sauce to taste. These make an adequate supper by themselves (a little Mexican beer wouldn't hurt!).

Taco Pie

Serves: 6
Prepare: 20 min.
Bake: 25–30 min.

Goes over BIG with teenagers!

1 pound lean ground beef
1 small onion, chopped
8 ounces tomato sauce
1 1¼-ounce package taco
  seasoning mix
⅓ cup chopped black olives
1 8-ounce can crescent
  roll dough

1½–2 cups crushed
  corn chips
1 cup light sour cream
1 cup shredded cheddar
  cheese

Preheat oven to 375°. Brown beef and onions over medium heat. Pour off any fat. Stir in tomato sauce, taco seasoning, and olives.

Unroll crescent roll dough to cover bottom of ungreased, shallow, 9×13-inch, baking dish, gently patting the perforated seams together. Sprinkle 1 cup of the crushed corn chips on top of dough. Spoon on meat mixture, then spread with sour cream. Add cheese and remaining crushed chips. Bake 25–30 minutes. Serve with the following ingredients, combined into a sauce.

2 tomatoes, chopped
2 avocados, diced
1 small onion, chopped
1 4-ounce can chopped
  green chilies

Juice of half a lemon
1 cup light sour cream
Salt to taste

Mexican-style Lasagne

Serves: 8
Prepare: 20 min.
Bake: 30 min.

One of our favorite family supper dishes . . .
easily cut in half to serve four.

2 pounds lean ground beef
1 1½-ounce package
  spaghetti sauce mix
1 teaspoon salt
2 15-ounce cans diced
  tomatoes in puree
1 cup water

1 4-ounce can diced
  green chilies
1 pound ricotta cheese
2 eggs, lightly beaten
8 corn tortillas
1 pound Monterey jack
  cheese, shredded

Preheat oven to 350°. In a heavy skillet, brown beef and drain fat. Add spaghetti sauce mix, salt, tomatoes, water, and chilies. Simmer 10 minutes. Combine ricotta cheese with eggs.

Place 1 cup of meat mixture in bottom of 9×12-inch (3-quart) baking dish. Top with 2 tortillas, side by side. Spoon ¼ of ricotta mixture onto each tortilla plus another layer of meat, sprinkling with ¼ of jack cheese. Repeat, using all of tortillas and ending with grated cheese.

Bake 30 minutes, uncovered. Let stand 5 minutes before cutting each stack into quarters.

If reducing recipe to half, use 1 tortilla at a time in a 9-inch pie plate.

Mexican-style Pizza

Serves: 4 to 6
Prepare: 30 min.
Bake: 20 min.

The perfect family supper.

Pizza Dough

1½ cups flour
½ cup white or yellow
  cornmeal (we preferred
  white)
1 tablespoon baking
  powder

1 teaspoon salt
⅓ cup shortening
¾ cup milk

Combine flour, cornmeal, baking powder, and salt. With a pastry blender, cut in shortening until mixture resembles fine crumbs. With a fork, stir in milk until dough forms and turn on to well-floured surface. Knead until dough is smooth, about 10 to 12 times.

Roll dough into 13-inch circle. Fold into quarters to place on an ungreased cookie sheet or pizza pan, then unfold. Pinch edge up to form a 1-inch rim.

Pizza Topping

1 pound lean ground beef
1 clove garlic, minced
1 16-ounce can
  refried beans
1 bunch green onions,
  chopped
1 4-ounce can chopped
  green chilies, drained

1 7 to 9-ounce bottle mild
  taco sauce
8–12 ounces (2–3 cups)
  shredded Monterey jack
  and cheddar cheeses

Preheat oven to 400°. Brown ground beef and garlic over medium heat. Drain well. Cover pizza dough with refried beans, using fingers to spread if too stiff. Layer beef mixture, chilies, taco sauce, and cheeses on top of beans.

Bake at 400° for 20 minutes. To serve, top with any or all of these garnishes:

shredded lettuce
chopped tomatoes
guacamole

sliced ripe olives
light sour cream

German Pot Roast

Serves: 8 to 12
Prepare: 25 min.
Bake: 2½–3 hours

This makes an unforgettable gravy.

8 pounds chuck roast
  (bone in)
Salt and pepper to taste
⅓ cup oil
1 onion sliced

3 carrots, diced
2 stalks celery, diced
1 leek, sliced
½ cup flour

Preheat oven to 375°. Salt and pepper meat. Heat oil in a heavy kettle or Dutch oven until very hot. Brown meat on all sides. Add vegetables and brown. Stir in flour to brown. ·

2 cups burgundy wine
3 fresh tomatoes, diced
  (or 1 16-ounce can)
1 10½-ounce can
  tomato puree
2 cloves garlic, minced

1 tablespoon paprika
1 tablespoon celery salt
1 bay leaf
¼ teaspoon basil
1½ quarts beef broth

Combine above ingredients and pour over meat. Bring to a gentle boil, skimming fat. Cover tightly and bake at 375° for 2½–3 hours, or until meat is tender.

Strain sauce through a sieve and serve with sliced meat and *Potato Pancakes*.

Sauerbraten

Serves: 8 to 12
Prepare: 15 min.
Simmer: 2½–3 hours
30 min.

Good German cooks, please look the other way! This version saves 3 days of waiting for a delicious dinner. Serve with applesauce, sour cream, and Potato Pancakes.

4 pounds boneless
   rump roast
Salt and pepper
2–3 tablespoons flour
2 tablespoons oil
2 tablespoons pickling
   spices

2 large onions, sliced
1 cup water
½ cup vinegar
2 tablespoons lemon juice
2 tablespoons catsup
6 gingersnaps

Dry meat with paper toweling. Sprinkle with salt and pepper; rub in flour. In a heavy Dutch oven, heat oil until hot, then brown meat on all sides.

Tie pickling spices up in cheesecloth. Add to meat with remaining ingredients, except gingersnaps. Cover pot and simmer 2½–3 hours.

Crumble gingersnaps into gravy and simmer another 30 minutes, until well-thickened and flavored. Remove spices before serving.

Carbonnade Flamande

Serves: 4 to 5
Prepare: 45 min.
Bake: 1½–2 hours
Chill: overnight

"My aunt, who lives in Brussels, gave me the recipe when I visited her in 1972." In testing, we thought this to be superior to any you might find in standard cookbooks. Do make it a day ahead to strengthen flavors. (A good dish to take to ski country!)

3 pounds boneless chuck, cut in thin 2×4-inch strips
¼–½ cup salad oil
4 large onions, thinly sliced
2 tablespoons brown sugar
1 cup beef stock or bouillon
1 clove garlic, minced
1 bay leaf
½ teaspoon thyme
¼ teaspoon nutmeg
1 teaspoon salt
3 cups beer
5 slices French bread
Dijon mustard

Preheat oven to 325°. Pat meat dry in paper toweling. In heavy Dutch oven or casserole, brown meat in oil over medium-high heat, in 2 to 3 batches. Set meat aside, and brown onions over medium heat. When tender, sprinkle with brown sugar and stir for another 2–3 minutes. Return meat to casserole and add broth, garlic, herbs, and salt. Pour in enough beer to completely cover meat.

Spread one side of bread slices with mustard. Place bread on top of meat, mustard-side-down. (The bread acts as a thickening agent, slowly dissolving in the cooking process.) Bring dish to a simmer, cover, and bake 1½–2 hours, until liquid is reduced to half. (If lid does not have a steamhole, leave partially askew.) Cool and refrigerate overnight, or freeze until later.

2 tablespoons vinegar
Salt and pepper to taste
2 tablespoons chopped parsley

To serve, reheat and stir in vinegar, and salt and pepper to taste. Sprinkle with parsley. Serve with buttered noodles, baby carrots, and *Green Beans with Tomatoes and Bacon.*

Rinderrouladen

Serves: 4 to 6
Prepare: 30 min.
Simmer: 1½ hours

Translated, these are "Beef Rolls"; a hearty dinner of rich flavors.

2–2½ pounds top round or
   sirloin tip
Dijon mustard
Salt
1–2 dill pickles, thinly sliced
1–2 carrots, thinly sliced
Onion slices

2–3 slices bacon, quartered
Oil
2–3 cups hot beef broth
4 peppercorns
½ bay leaf
3 tablespoons cornstarch
3 tablespoons cold water

It would be nice if you could persuade your butcher to cut ¼-inch thick slices from the top round. Depending on size, you should have 2–3 slices per person.

Spread each piece of meat with Dijon mustard and sprinkle with salt. At the small end, place thin slices of pickle, carrot, onion, and bacon. Roll up and close with toothpicks.

In a Dutch oven, brown rolls in a small amount of oil over medium-high heat. Add hot beef broth, peppercorns, and bay leaf. Simmer, covered, for 1½ hours or until beef rolls are tender.

Remove beef rolls to warm platter. Remove bay leaf. Make a paste of the cornstarch and cold water. Stir into broth with a whisk and simmer until thickened. You may have to make more cornstarch paste, depending on amount of broth and desired thickness. Serve with beef rolls.

Spaetzle noodles are very good with this (they are now readily found in supermarkets), plus *Danish Red Cabbage* and *Butter Lettuce and Egg Salad.*

Tyrolean Liver

Serves: 4
Prepare: 20 min.

We were a little shy about the pickle and capers, but they turned out to be the keys to this delicious recipe. Our skier donor brought this to us from Aspen via a Kitzbühel skier! She says, "It's so simple to prepare while your guests are sipping whatever . . . ."

1 pound calves liver, cut in 2-inch wide strips
Flour
3 tablespoons oil
½ cup finely chopped onion
¼ cup beef stock
1 sour pickle, finely chopped

2–3 tablespoons capers
2 tablespoons chopped chives
2 tablespoons chopped parsley
1–1½ cups light sour cream

Very lightly coat liver strips with flour, then brown quickly in hot oil. Remove liver from skillet, reduce heat, then sauté onion until soft. Return meat to pan with stock and bring to a simmer. Add remaining ingredients and reheat, but do not boil.

Serve with noodles or rice, salad greens, and that favorite bottle of red wine.

Pasta, Eggs, Cheese, and Rice

Green Chile Pasta

Serves: 6
Prepare: 10 min.
Cook: 15 min.

Great with steaks!...or almost anything bar-becued. Another ideal recipe for the galley.

6 slices bacon, diced
8 ounces uncooked vermi-celli or thin spaghetti
1 large onion, chopped
1 14½-ounce can regular-strength beef broth
1 16-ounce can tomatoes

1 4-ounce can diced green chilies
2 tablespoons red wine vinegar
Salt and pepper to taste
Freshly grated Parmesan cheese

Sauté bacon pieces in a Dutch oven until crisp. Remove and drain, reserving ¼ cup bacon drippings in pan.

Break pasta into 2-inch pieces and stir into bacon fat over medium heat. Add onion and sauté until golden. Add beef broth, tomatoes (breaking up with a spoon), chilies, and vinegar. Stir well.

Cover and simmer until spaghetti is tender and most of liquid is absorbed; about 15 minutes.

To serve, sprinkle bacon pieces on top and pass grated cheese. As a supper dish, all you need with this is crusty bread and tossed greens.

Chiles Relleños

Serves: 4 to 6
Prepare: 15 min.
Bake: 1 hour

You'll have a hard time finding an easier or better version.

2–3 4-ounce cans
   whole green chilies
6 large eggs
⅔ cup flour
1 cup light cream

8 ounces Monterey jack
   cheese, grated
8 ounces sharp cheddar
   cheese, grated
1 8-ounce can tomato sauce

Preheat oven to 325°. Rinse and remove seeds and fibers from chilies. Drain on paper towels.

With a beater or whisk, beat eggs and flour until smooth and add cream. Lightly spray a shallow, 9×13-inch casserole with vegetable oil. Layer egg mixture, chilies, and cheeses. Top with tomato sauce.

Bake, uncovered, for 1 hour. Serve with a tossed green salad and hot, crusty bread; or really "go Mexican" with refried beans, Spanish rice, and warm flour tortillas.

Sausage and Spinach Frittata

Serves: 6
Prepare: 20 min.
Bake: 25–30 min.

Frittatas are fun because no two have to be alike and yet the ingredients and preparation are easy. This one is done in the oven, and you may substitute barely cooked zucchini or broccoli for the spinach.

½ pound fresh spinach
   (or 1 10-ounce package
   frozen)
1 or 2 Italian sausages
1 tablespoon oil

1 tablespoon butter
1 medium onion, chopped
2 cloves garlic, minced
⅓–½ pound mushrooms,
   sliced

Preheat oven to 350°. If using fresh spinach, wash and cook in just the water that clings to the leaves. When just tender, drain well and squeeze until free of all moisture. Coarsley chop. (If using frozen spinach, you do not need to cook after thawing.)

Remove casings from sausages. Crumble and sauté in a skillet until brown. Remove sausage to paper toweling to drain, and clean skillet of fat. Heat oil and butter, then sauté onion, garlic, and mushrooms until onion is translucent. Remove from heat and stir in drained spinach.

6 eggs
¾ cup grated Parmesan
   cheese
½ teaspoon basil
¼ teaspoon marjoram
½ teaspoon salt

Freshly ground pepper
   to taste
1 cup (4 ounces) shredded
   mozzarella cheese
¼ cup grated Parmesan
   cheese

In medium-size bowl, lightly beat eggs with a whisk then add ¾ cup Parmesan cheese and seasonings. Stir in sausage and vege-tables. Pour into buttered 9-inch pie plate. Sprinkle with mozzarella cheese and rest of Parmesan. Bake at 350° for 25–30 minutes, or until set. Bread sticks and a green salad will complete the supper.

Boboli with Feta Cheese

Serves: 4
Prepare: 15 min.
Bake: 10 min.

Boboli cheese pizza crusts not only do wonders facilitating a speedy, nutritious meal but they can bring out the creative genius in even the most timid cook. Here's one delicious version.

4 4-ounce Boboli (Italian bread shells)
Olive oil
½ cup finely chopped Greek olives or sun-dried tomatoes
1 large red onion, thinly sliced

8 ounces feta cheese (or any favorite goat cheese), crumbled
1 teaspoon olive oil
¼ cup pine nuts or chopped walnuts
¼ cup fresh oregano leaves, left whole or coarsely chopped

Preheat oven to 450°. Place Boboli shells on a foil-lined cookie sheet, and brush the tops lightly with olive oil. Spread the chopped olives or sun-dried tomatoes over shells.

Place sliced red onions in a microwave-safe dish and microwave on high for 20 seconds. (Or sauté in a touch of oil until barely softened.) Divide the onions among the shells, and top with crumbled cheese.

Place the pizzas on the middle rack of the preheated oven and bake until the cheese softens; about 10 minutes.

Meanwhile, in a small skillet, lightly sauté nuts in a teaspoon of olive oil until they just begin to turn a toasty brown. Remove from heat.

When pizzas are done top with the toasted nuts and fresh oregano leaves. Cut into quarters and serve immediately.

Rice and Green Chilies Cheese Bake

Serves: 8
Prepare: 35 min.
Bake: 45 min.

An excellent vegetarian entree that pleases the pocketbook, too.

1 cup brown rice
3 medium zucchini, thinly sliced
8 ounces tomato sauce with basil
1 7½-ounce can whole green chilies, deveined, seeded, and chopped
12 ounces Monterey jack cheese, grated

1 large tomato, thinly sliced
2 cups light sour cream
½ cup chopped green onion
¼ cup chopped green pepper
1 teaspoon oregano
1 teaspoon garlic salt
2 tablespoons chopped parsley

Prepare rice according to package directions. Place zucchini slices in a skillet with a small amount of water. Lightly salt and pepper, then tightly cover and cook over medium heat until barely tender; about 2–3 minutes. Drain well.

Preheat oven to 350°. Combine tomato sauce and rice and place in a buttered, shallow, 3-quart casserole. Cover with chopped chilies and half of grated cheese. Arrange zucchini slices over cheese, then top with tomato slices. Salt to taste.

Combine remaining ingredients, except parsley, and spoon evenly over tomato layer. Cover with remaining cheese.

Bake, uncovered, for 45–50 minutes, or until heated through and bubbly. Sprinkle with parsley and serve with a crisp green salad and whole wheat rolls or French bread.

Pete White's Savory Rice

Serves: 6
Prepare: 15 min.
Cook: 30 min.

No one seems to remember who Pete White is, but his rice is certainly memorable. It's excellent with Eddy's Chicken Kiev *or almost any barbecued meat.*

2 onions, chopped
3 tablespoons butter
1 cup long-grain white rice
1 teaspoon marjoram
1 teaspoon rosemary, crumbled

½ teaspoon summer savory
1 10½-ounce can consommé or chicken broth
1½ cups water

In a large, heavy saucepan, sauté onions in butter until transparent. Add rice and herbs. Continue sautéing until rice is lightly browned, stirring frequently. Add consommé and water. Simmer, covered, for 30 minutes or until rice is tender and moisture absorbed.

Brown Rice Pilaf

Serves: 6
Prepare: 10 min.
Cook: 40–45 min.

The white raisins and spices do neat things for this recipe. Excellent with roast pork and lamb.

2½ cups chicken broth
1 cup long grain brown rice, rinsed
1 tablespoon oil
1 tablespoon butter
1 green pepper, chopped
1 medium onion, chopped
1 celery stalk, finely chopped

⅔ cup white raisins
1 teaspoon powdered ginger
Pinch of curry powder
Pinch of ground cloves
Salt and pepper to taste

Bring broth to boil, add rice. Reduce heat and simmer, covered, until liquid is absorbed; about 40–45 minutes.

Heat oil and butter in a skillet. Sauté green pepper, onion, and celery until limp. Stir in raisins and spices. Add to cooked rice. Season with salt and pepper to taste.

Note: If making ahead, add more chicken broth to reheat.

Lida's Wild Rice

Serves: 6 to 8
Prepare: 10 min.
Soak: 8 hours
Cook: 30 min.
Steam: 1 hour

"A special friend from Minnesota gave this recipe to us years ago . . .the steaming is the secret."

½ pound (1⅓ cups)
  wild rice
2 cups undiluted beef
  consommé
  (or chicken broth)*
1 clove garlic

Rinse rice and soak in cold water overnight or for at least 8 hours. Rinse thoroughly then simmer, covered, in consommé with a clove of garlic for 30 minutes, or until all liquid is absorbed. Discard garlic.

1 large onion, chopped
½ pound mushrooms,
  sliced
2 tablespoons butter

¼ cup dry sherry
Salt and pepper to taste
Butter

Sauté onion and mushrooms in 2 tablespoons butter until soft. Place in top of double boiler with cooked rice and sherry. Add salt, pepper, and butter to taste.

One hour before serving, steam rice mixture in top of covered double boiler . . .even a little longer won't hurt! Needless to say, this is super with *Skagit Valley Wild Duck.*

Note: Use chicken broth if you do not wish the dish to compete with a mildly flavored entree.

100

Vegetables
and
Complements

Baked Potato Wedges

Serves: 4 to 6
Prepare: 10 min.
Bake: 35 min.

A really nice change in potato recipes.

4 tablespoons butter,
  melted
¼ cup catsup
1 teaspoon prepared
  mustard
½ teaspoon paprika
¼ teaspoon salt
¼ teaspoon freshly
  ground pepper
4 large potatoes, unpeeled

Preheat oven to 425°. Combine melted butter, catsup, mustard, and seasonings.

Scrub potatoes and dry well. Cut each into 4 wedges. Slash each wedge crosswise at ¼-inch intervals, but *don't* cut through skin. Place wedges on a foil-lined cookie sheet, skin-side down. Brush with ⅓ of butter mixture.

Bake 35–40 minutes or until potatoes are fork-tender, basting periodically with remaining butter mixture.

Light Sour Cream Potatoes

Serves: 4
Prepare: 10 min.
Cook: 15 min.

A very attractive, easy, healthful way to serve potatoes . . . excellent with barbecued flank steak.

4–6 medium red-skinned
   potatoes
1 small onion, minced
1 teaspoon salt
1 generous grinding of
   black pepper
½ cup boiling water
¼ cup light sour cream
Chopped chives or parsley

Scrub potatoes but do not peel; cut into ¾-inch cubes. Place in skillet with onion, seasonings, and boiling water. Return to a boil, cover, and simmer 10–15 minutes until tender. Do not drain.

Add sour cream. Toss lightly and pour into heated serving dish. Sprinkle generously with chopped chives or parsley.

Potatoes Dauphinoise

Serves: 4
Prepare: 15 min.
Bake: 45 min.

A delicious refinement of scalloped potatoes that can be made ahead of time except for baking.

1½ pounds potatoes
  (3 medium-large)
2 cups milk
2 eggs, well-beaten
Salt to taste
¼ teaspoon freshly
  ground pepper

Grating of nutmeg
1½ cups (6 ounces) grated,
  semi-soft cheese such as
  Babybel or Bonybel
1 clove garlic, split
2 tablespoons butter

Preheat oven to 350°. Peel and very thinly slice potatoes into cold water to prevent darkening. Combine milk with beaten eggs, salt, pepper, and nutmeg. Stir in half of grated cheese.

Rub a 1½-quart casserole with split garlic, then grease with a teaspoon of the butter. Drain potatoes *very well* and place in casserole. Top with milk mixture. Sprinkle with remaining cheese and dot with rest of butter.

Bake at 350° for 40–45 minutes, or until potatoes are tender and top is well-browned.

Potato Pancakes

Serves: 8
Prepare: 15 min.

Ideal with German Pot Roast *or* Sauerbraten.

3 potatoes
2 eggs, beaten
¼ teaspoon nutmeg
1 tablespoon chopped
   parsley
2 tablespoons flour
½ teaspoon baking powder
Salt to taste
2 tablespoons butter
2 tablespoons oil

Finely shred or grate potatoes and immediately place in a bowl of cold water to prevent darkening. Beat together remaining ingredients, except butter and oil.

Heat butter and oil in heavy skillet. Squeeze potatoes between toweling to remove all excess moisture. Immediately combine with batter. Drop by tablespoonfuls into hot grease. Crisply brown on both sides, adding more oil if necessary. Keep warm in oven until ready to serve.

Sweet Potatoes with Rum

Serves: 8
Prepare: 20 min.
Bake: 20 min.

The sweet potatoes are whipped with just a touch of spice and rum to make them really special. Easily prepared a day ahead.

4 cups hot, cooked sweet
    potatoes
3 tablespoons butter
⅓–½ cup heavy cream
2 tablespoons rum
2 tablespoons brown sugar
½ teaspoon mace

½ teaspoon salt
¼ teaspoon white pepper
2 tablespoons chopped
    walnuts
1 tablespoon grated
    orange rind
1 tablespoon melted butter

Preheat oven to 375°. With an electric mixer, combine all of the ingredients except the nuts, orange rind, and melted butter. Beat until fluffy, adding a little more cream if necessary.

Pour into buttered, 1½-quart, deep casserole. Sprinkle with nuts and orange rind. Drizzle melted butter over top. Bake, uncovered, for 20 minutes.

Gingered Carrots

Serves: 6   *A wonderful blend of flavors.*
Prepare: 20 min.

7–8 medium carrots
1 tablespoon sugar
1 teaspoon cornstarch
¼ teaspoon salt
¼ teaspoon ground ginger
¼ cup orange juice
2 tablespoons butter
Chopped parsley

Cut carrots on the bias into ⅛ to ¼-inch thick slices. Cook, covered, in boiling salted water until just tender, about 7 to 10 minutes. Drain.

Meanwhile, combine sugar, cornstarch, salt, and ginger in a small saucepan. Add orange juice and cook, stirring constantly, until mixture thickens and bubbles. Boil 1 minute then stir in butter. Pour over hot carrots and toss. Garnish with chopped parsley.

These are really good with *Baked Chicken in Lemon* and broccoli or asparagus with *Hollandaise Sauce.* Can be made ahead and reheated.

Carrot and Cauliflower Medley

Serves: 8
Prepare: 25 min.
Bake: 15 min.

You'll find this a versatile vegetable dish, fitting into almost any menu . . .and it's good! Because it may be made ahead, it's ideal for buffets.

8 large carrots	1 cup chicken broth
1 large cauliflower head	½ cup heavy cream
2 tablespoons butter	1¼ cups shredded
2 tablespoons flour	Swiss cheese
½ teaspoon Dijon mustard	2–3 green onions, sliced

Cut carrots into ¼-inch thick slices. Break cauliflower into flowerets. Cook vegetables in boiling, salted water until just tender, approximately 5 minutes. Plunge into cold water and drain.

In a large saucepan, melt butter over medium heat. Stir in flour and mustard with a whisk, and cook until bubbly. Remove from heat and gradually stir in chicken broth and cream. Return to heat and cook, stirring, until thickened. Gradually add one cup of the cheese, reserving remaining ¼ cup. Stir until melted.

Combine vegetables and sauce in a buttered, 2-quart casserole. Sprinkle with remaining cheese. If done ahead, cover and refrigerate.

Preheat oven to 350°. Bake, uncovered, for 15–20 minutes (35 minutes, if chilled). Garnish with green onion slices.

Corn in Cream

Serves: 8
Prepare: 15 min.
Bake: 1½ hours

A simple, uncontrived vegetable dish that can be prepared ahead.

12 ears small-kernel corn
3 tablespoons chopped
   chives
1 tablespoon sugar
1½ teaspoons salt
¼ teaspoon ground white
   pepper
1–2 cups cream

Preheat oven to 300°. Using your sharpest knife, carefully slice off corn without cutting into cob. Use dull side of knife to scrape remaining pulp and juice from cob (the best part!).

    Combine with chives, sugar, salt, and pepper, and spoon into well-buttered, shallow, 9×13-inch baking dish. Add enough cream to cover corn. Bake, uncovered, for 1½ hours.

Fresh Spinach Casserole

Serves: 6
Prepare: 20 min.
Bake: 30 min.

A really nice way to prepare a fresh vegetable dish ahead of time for potlucks or buffets.

2½ pounds fresh spinach
1 teaspoon salt
2 tablespoons melted butter
2 eggs, lightly beaten
1 cup milk
1 tablespoon minced onion
½ teaspoon salt
⅛ teaspoon white pepper
Grating of nutmeg (optional)
½ cup shredded
    Swiss cheese

Thoroughly wash spinach. Place spinach in pot with only the water that clings to its leaves. Add 1 teaspoon salt, cover, and cook over moderate heat until barely tender, about 2 minutes. Drain, squeezing all water from spinach. Finely chop.

Combine well-drained spinach with remaining ingredients. Place in a buttered, shallow, 1-quart casserole. At this point, you may cover and refrigerate until baking time.

Bake, uncovered, at 325° until set; about 30 minutes (45 minutes, if refrigerated). It should be golden brown on top.

Baked Artichokes with Mushrooms

Serves: 6
Prepare: 20 min.
Bake: 30–40 min.

Not only is it good, but it adds a great touch of color to a menu. We particularly like it with simply prepared fish and buttered green peas.

6 slices bacon, diced
1 tablespoon butter
1 onion, chopped
2 8-ounce cans tomato
  sauce
1 pound mushrooms
3 tablespoons dry
  white wine

2 7-ounce cans
  artichoke hearts
2 tablespoons chopped
  pecans
2 tablespoons chopped
  parsley
2 tablespoons grated
  Parmesan cheese

Preheat oven to 350°. In a small skillet, sauté diced bacon and drain on paper toweling. Pour off grease, then melt butter in same skillet and gently sauté onion. When soft, stir in tomato sauce and simmer over low heat for several minutes. Set aside.

Clean mushrooms. Separate stems and caps, trimming base of stems. Chop stems (easy in a food processor), and add to tomato sauce. Either leave caps whole or slice, depending on desired appearance in dish. Set aside.

Butter a shallow, 8×12-inch baking dish and pour wine into bottom. Either leave artichoke hearts whole or quarter (again, according to desired appearance), and arrange in dish with mushroom caps. Pour tomato sauce over top, then sprinkle with bacon bits, chopped pecans, parsley, and Parmesan cheese. Bake, uncovered, at 350° until bubbly; about 30–40 minutes.

Gratin of Eggplant and Tomatoes

Serves: 6 to 8
Prepare: 25 min.
Bake: 15 min.

This may be treated as a vegetarian entree or reach the other end of the spectrum and be served with roast beef. No matter what, it's delicious.

3 tablespoons butter
½ small onion, minced
2 pounds ripe tomatoes,
   peeled, seeded, and diced
¼ cup heavy cream
1 teaspoon salt
¼ teaspoon pepper
¼ teaspoon sugar

2 large eggplants,
   peeled and sliced
Flour
Butter
¼–½ cup grated Parmesan
   cheese
12 ounces mozzarella
   cheese, shredded

Melt 3 tablespoons butter in large sauce pan and sauté onion until golden. Add diced tomatoes, cooking until soft. Stir in cream, salt, pepper, and sugar. Set aside.

Season eggplant slices with salt and pepper and dip in flour. Sauté both sides in butter until soft. Drain on paper towels.

Arrange half of eggplant in ungreased, 9×13-inch shallow baking dish. Cover with half of tomato mixture, half of grated Parmesan, and half of mozzarella. Repeat. At this point, dish may be set aside or refrigerated until ready to bake.

Preheat oven to 450°. Bake, uncovered, until sauce bubbles and cheese is melted; about 15 minutes, unchilled, or 25 minutes, chilled.

Our vegetarian tester served this with toasted, homemade, whole wheat bread and fresh asparagus.

Eggplant and Rice Provençal

Serves: 8
Prepare: 30 min.
Bake: 45 min.

We urge you to try this, even if you are not an eggplant enthusiast. It's a very pretty casserole that can be made ahead and served as a main course or as company to such good things as Crayfish or barbecued salmon.

1 large eggplant, unpeeled
¼ cup olive oil
3 cups chopped onion
1 green pepper, cut in
   1-inch squares
2 cloves garlic, minced
1 teaspoon oregano,
   crumbled

1 bay leaf
3 tomatoes, chopped
1 cup raw rice*
3¼ cups chicken broth
Salt and pepper to taste
½ cup grated Parmesan
   cheese
2 tablespoons butter

Preheat oven to 350°. Cut eggplant into 1-inch cubes. In a large heavy skillet, heat oil and add eggplant. Stir and sauté over high heat until soft. Add onion, green pepper, garlic, and herbs, and cook until onions are soft. Stir in tomatoes, lower heat, and simmer 5 minutes or until most of liquid has evaporated.

Stir in rice and chicken broth. Season with salt and pepper to taste. Spoon into a buttered, deep, 3-quart baking dish. Sprinkle with Parmesan cheese and dot with butter.

Bake, uncovered, for 45 minutes to one hour, or until rice is done. *(If using brown rice, increase baking time by 15 minutes.)

Sautéed Leeks with Tomatoes

Serves: 4 to 6
Prepare: 15 min.
Cook: 5 min.

The leeks have such a marvelous, delicate flavor that there's no need for special seasoning. This is a colorful vegetable dish that may be prepared ahead.

3 or 4 large leeks
2 or 3 medium-size
  tomatoes
1 tablespoon butter
1 tablespoon oil
Salt and freshly
  ground pepper

Trim tough ends from leeks, leaving tenderer part of green for color. Cut in 3 to 4-inch lengths, then quarter lengthwise. Rinse well.

Plunge tomatoes into boiling water for 1 minute to split skins, then peel. Quarter, being careful to retain juice.

Heat butter and oil in a heavy skillet over medium to low heat. Add leeks and sauté for 2–3 minutes until they soften, turning frequently. When golden, add juicy tomato quarters and continue stirring until vegetables are nicely blended and heated through. Add salt and freshly ground pepper to taste. This is best served immediately, but is still delicious gently reheated.

Green Beans with Tomatoes and Bacon

Serves: 4
Prepare: 10 min.

Bright colors, bright flavors. Can be made ahead in quantity for a group...maybe a salmon barbeque?

1 10-ounce package frozen
  cut green beans
2 slices bacon, diced
1 tablespoon bacon
  drippings
¼ cup chopped onion

1 medium tomato, diced
1½–2 tablespoons cider
  vinegar
¼ teaspoon sugar
⅛ teaspoon salt

Cook frozen beans in a small amount of lightly salted water for only a minute past thawing stage. They must remain tender-crisp and bright green. Drain.

In a skillet, sauté diced bacon until crisp. Remove to a paper towel to drain. Reserve 1 tablespoon of bacon drippings in pan. Sauté onion until limp. Add diced tomato, and sprinkle with vinegar and seasonings. Cook, stirring gently, only until heated through and tomatoes have softened. Add beans to heat through. Toss with bacon and serve.

If you wish to prepare ahead, plunge just-cooked beans in cold water, drain and refrigerate in a plastic bag. Prepare bacon and tomato mixture. A few minutes before serving, reheat beans and tomato mixture and toss with bacon.

Green Beans al Pesto

Serves: 6
Prepare: 15 min.

The pesto flavor turns green beans into an elegant vegetable or salad course. Read on for all the variables.

1–1½ pounds fresh
  green beans
½ cup chopped
  green onions
2 tablespoons chopped
  parsley
2 tablespoons chopped
  fresh basil

2–2½ tablespoons
  lemon juice
½ cup walnuts
½–¾ cup olive oil
Salt and pepper to taste

Wash and trim beans. Leave whole, if serving as a salad. Otherwise, slice as desired. In 3–4 quarts boiling, salted water, add beans and cover just to return boil. Uncover and gently boil 5–6 minutes, or until beans are tender but still crisp. Do not overcook.

If not serving hot, plunge beans in icy, cold water to stop cooking process and retain color.

To make sauce, place rest of ingredients (start out with ½ cup oil) in blender jar. Blend until smooth (a few chunks of walnuts add something, though). Add more oil, if necessary.

If serving beans hot, pour sauce over and serve immediately. As a salad course, marinate beans in sauce for at least an hour.

Variations: Try with cold, rigatoni noodles and a package of frozen peas; marinate several hours or so. Dress up even more for a luncheon salad or summer evening, by adding seafood.

Zucchini Creole

Serves: 6 to 8
Prepare: 10 min.
Bake: 1 hour

One of those dishes that works with almost anything, and you'll barely know you're in the kitchen.

3 tablespoons butter
3 tablespoons flour
1 16-ounce can stewed
  tomatoes
1 tablespoon brown sugar

½ bay leaf
2 cloves
Salt to taste
6 medium zucchini, sliced

Preheat oven to 350°. Melt butter in a large saucepan. Stir in flour with a whisk until smooth and bubbly. Add remaining ingredients except zucchini and simmer, uncovered, for 5 minutes.

Place sliced zucchini in ungreased, 2-quart, baking dish. Pour sauce over and bake, uncovered, 1 hour.

Zucchini and Mushrooms

Serves: 8
Prepare: 25 min.
Bake: 20 min.

A very tasty entree or side dish.

8 medium zucchini
½ cup butter
1 medium onion, finely chopped
1 pound mushrooms, minced
1 teaspoon salt

Freshly ground pepper to taste
1 cup soft bread crumbs
1 clove garlic, minced
1 cup shredded Gruyère cheese

Preheat oven to 350°. Cut zucchini in half, cross-wise. Either steam on a rack, or stand upright in Dutch oven or large sauce pan and simmer, covered, in salted water for 5 minutes. Drain, cool, and cut in half, lengthwise. Gently scoop out seeds and pulp and puree in a food processor, reserving shells.

In a large skillet, melt butter and sauté onion until clear. Add mushrooms and sauté until soft. Season with salt and pepper. Remove from heat and add bread crumbs, garlic, half of the grated cheese, and the zucchini pulp, mixing well.

Heap mixture into zucchini shells and place in a buttered, shallow, 3-quart baking dish. Sprinkle with remaining cheese. (Dot with additional butter, if you wish.) Bake at 350° for 20 minutes or until golden brown.

As a vegetarian entree, serve with a Caesar salad and French bread. As a side dish, it's perfect with *Grilled Chicken Breasts in Red Wine* and baked potatoes.

Sassy Zucchini

Serves: 6
Prepare: 20 min.
Broil: 10 min.

This can make a beautiful vegetable dish by using it to surround Gingered Carrots, *or is delicious by itself as company to chicken or meats. Try it as a fun h'ors d'oeuvre.*

1½–2 pounds zucchini, unpeeled
⅔ cup mayonnaise
¼ cup grated Parmesan cheese
2 tablespoons crumbled blue cheese
¼ teaspoon garlic salt

Slice zucchini into ¼-inch thick rounds and place on foil-lined cookie sheet. Combine remaining ingredients and mound by the teaspoonful on each zucchini slice. Broil at low temperature, with rack set about midway in oven. Serve when lightly browned.

Fried Apples

Serves: 4 to 8
Prepare: 15–20 min.

An unusual accent for roast pork or Stuffed Pork Chops, *with a caramel-like taste and texture.*

½ cup butter
¾ pound brown sugar
¼ cup vinegar
4–6 cooking apples*

In a large, heavy skillet, melt butter and stir in brown sugar and vinegar. Heat until bubbling.

*Using only apples that will remain firm when cooked, peel, core, and slice 1–1½ inches thick. Lay in bubbling syrup and cook until brown and caramelized, being careful not to burn. They should be tender when touched with a fork.

Danish Red Cabbage

Serves: 8 to 10
Prepare: 10 min.
Cook: 45 min.

Notice the currant jelly. That's what makes this so good.

1 small head red cabbage
1 tablespoon butter
½ cup cider vinegar
¼ cup currant jelly
¼ cup sugar
1 teaspoon salt

Finely shred cabbage (ideal in a food processor). In a large sauce pan or small Dutch oven, melt butter and add remaining ingredients. Bring to a simmer, then add cabbage. Cover and cook gently until tender, about 45 minutes.

This may be served hot or cold and is even better the next day. Our Danish donor says that it is traditional for her Christmas goose dinner, but is delicious with many things such as sausages, turkey, roast beef, and marinated meats.

Baked Cranberry Relish

Serves: 8
Prepare: 10 min.
Bake: 1¼ hours

It's the simplicity of this recipe that makes it so good. A great color accent when prepared in a stark-white, baking dish.

1 quart raw cranberries, washed
1½ cups sugar
1 teaspoon cinnamon
½ cup broken walnuts or pecans

Preheat oven to 275°. Combine berries with sugar in ungreased, deep, 1½-quart baking dish. Bake, uncovered, until berries become juicy; about 1 hour.

Increase oven temperature to 350°. Sprinkle cinnamon over top of berries, cover, and bake until berries are clear but still whole; about 15 minutes.

Sprinkle nuts on top and serve warm with roast pork or turkey.

Note: This will keep a week or more in refrigerator.

Mustard Cream

Yield: 2½ cups
Prepare: 5 min.

Wonderful! Serve with ham or barbequed chicken or Scotch Eggs.

1 cup sugar
2 tablespoons dry mustard
1 tablespoon flour or
   cornstarch

1 egg yolk
½ cup vinegar
1 cup cream

In 1-quart saucepan, combine all ingredients with a whisk. Bring to a boil, stirring constantly. Remove and cool.

Mustard Sauce

Yield: 3 cups
Prepare: 5 min.
Stand: overnight

It's hot and full-flavored . . .ideal for Skagit Valley Wild Duck.

1 cup dry mustard
1 cup cider vinegar
3 eggs, lightly beaten
1 cup sugar

Whisk together mustard and vinegar. Let stand in a covered bowl overnight.

   In top of double boiler, combine egg and sugar. Add mustard mixture, blending well. Cook over boiling water, stirring constantly until thick.

Hollandaise Sauce

Yield: 1¼ cups
Prepare: 3 min.

This method is so easy, speedy, and foolproof.

½ pound butter
4 egg yolks
2 tablespoons lemon juice
Pinch of cayenne pepper

Melt butter until just bubbling. Place remaining ingredients in electric blender. Cover and turn on to high speed. Remove cover and add hot butter in a steady stream.

This may be made ahead and kept at room temperature for several hours or refrigerated, then set over warm water to return to proper consistency.

Is there anything better over broccoli or asparagus? Add a teaspoon of dried tarragon to serve with poached or baked salmon.

Sauce for Salmon

Yield: 1¾ cups
Prepare: 5 min.
Chill: 2 hours

The capers and the curry make this very special. It would be equally good on a crab-meat salad . . .even more fun at cocktail time as a topping for tiny, boiled, red potatoes.

1½ cups mayonnaise
2 teaspoons curry powder
1 tablespoon grated onion
3–4 tablespoons
    drained capers
2–3 drops Tabasco sauce
¼ cup finely chopped
    parsley

Combine all ingredients and chill for 2 hours or more. Serve with cold salmon.

Breads,
Pancakes,
and
Coffee Cakes

Camembert French Bread

Serves: 6 to 8
Prepare: 10 min.
Cool: 10 min.
Bake: 5 min.

Just the right thing with a steak dinner.

4 ounces Camembert cheese	½ teaspoon onion or garlic salt
½ cup butter	1 large loaf French Bread
¼ teaspoon dried basil	

Remove casing from cheese. Combine in a saucepan with butter, basil, and onion or garlic salt. Stir over low heat for 5 minutes, until thoroughly blended. Cool 10 minutes, stirring occasionally.

Slice bread in half lengthwise. Spread half of cheese mixture on cut surfaces. Reassemble and spread rest of mixture on top and sides of loaf. Set loaf in a pan of foil and bake in a 375° oven for 5 minutes. Slice and serve hot.

Thomas Bröd

Yield: 2 loaves
Prepare: 10 min.
Bake: 1 hour

This Swedish recipe was imported and adapted by one of our more ardent cooks and testers. Once you have acquired goodly supplies of the basic ingredients from health food or specialty stores, keep them in canisters for spur-of-the-moment baking.

2 cups rye flour
(or ½ rye, ½ white)
2 cups whole wheat flour
1 cup wheat germ
1 cup Scott's Oats (a
Scottish product sold in
specialty food stores)

¾ cup cracked wheat
4 teaspoons baking powder
1 teaspoon salt
1 quart buttermilk
¾ cup dark Karo syrup

Preheat oven to 350°. Combine dry ingredients, then stir in buttermilk and Karo syrup until well-blended. Divide between 2 greased loaf pans. Bake 1 hour (do not expect much rising).

Marvelously wholesome and nutty in flavor, you'll love it with *Canadian Cheese Soup* or as a snack with thin slices of Swiss cheese . . .even better yet, toasted with honey.

Zucchini Bread

Yield: 2 loaves
Prepare: 15 min.
Bake: 1 hour

It's not just another zucchini bread recipe . . .
this one will take the blue ribbon.

3 eggs
2 cups sugar
1 cup salad oil
1 tablespoon vanilla
2 cups grated, unpeeled
  zucchini (loosely packed)
2 cups unbleached flour
1 tablespoon cinnamon
2 teaspoons baking soda
1 teaspoon salt
½ teaspoon baking powder
1 cup chopped walnuts
½ cup sesame seeds
  (optional)

Preheat oven to 350°. In a large bowl, beat eggs until frothy. Beat in sugar, oil, and vanilla until thick and lemon-colored. Stir in zucchini.

Sift together flour, cinnamon, baking soda, salt, and baking powder. Stir into zucchini batter. Fold in walnuts. Pour mixture into 2 oiled, 9-inch, loaf pans. Sprinkle sesame seeds on top and bake 1 hour. Let cool 10 minutes before turning out on rack.

Banana Bread

Yield: 1 loaf
Prepare: 10 min.
Bake: 1 hour, 20 min.

Would any cookbook be complete without a recipe for banana bread? This one makes a high, cake-like loaf that's still moist and just wonderful, and there's no way you can "goof"!

2 ripe bananas
1½ cups sugar
2 eggs
½ cup vegetable oil
1¾ cups flour
1 teaspoon baking soda

½ teaspoon salt
¼ cup plus 1 tablespoon buttermilk
1 teaspoon vanilla
1 cup chopped pecans

Preheat oven to 325°. In large mixing bowl, mash bananas. Beat in sugar, eggs, and oil. Sift together flour, baking soda, and salt. Mix into batter with remaining ingredients.

Pour into greased, 9×5-inch, loaf pan. Bake 1 hour and 20–30 minutes, until golden brown and top splits. Cool on rack 20 minutes before removing from pan.

Cranberry Bread

Yield: 1 loaf
Prepare: 20 min.
Bake: 1 hour

This recipe originated from a charming children's book, "Cranberry Thanksgiving". In the story, the villain tries to steal the recipe . . . we're glad we stole it!

2 cups flour
1 cup sugar
1¼ teaspoons baking powder
½ teaspoon baking soda
1 teaspoon salt
¼ cup butter, softened

1 egg, beaten
1 teaspoon grated orange peel
¾ cup orange juice
2 cups chopped cranberries

Preheat oven to 350°. Combine dry ingredients. Cut in butter. Add egg, orange peel and juice. Mix well, then stir in cranberries. Pour into greased loaf pan. Bake 1 hour. (Recipe may easily be doubled.)

Butterhorns

Yield: 20 to 40 rolls
Prepare: 10 min.
Chill (optional)
Bake: 20–30 min.

You'll be crazy about this recipe. It's wonderfully versatile . . .a scrumptious breakfast treat or fanciful hors d'oeuvre or dainty dinner roll.

2 cups flour
2 cups small-curd
   cottage cheese
1 cup butter, softened

Combine above ingredients with a spoon. Divide into two equal portions, wrap in plastic film, and chill until firm. (If kitchen is cool enough and you use a pastry cloth, this is not necessary.)

Preheat oven to 375°. On lightly floured board, roll out each portion into ⅛-inch thick circle. Cut circles into fourths, then each fourth into 5 wedges (20 wedges per circle). Starting at bigger end, roll wedges up and place on ungreased cookie sheet, seam-side down and forming a crescent. Bake on middle rack of oven for 20-30 minutes, until lightly browned. Cool ten minutes.

1 cup powdered sugar
1–2 tablespoons cream
   or milk
½ teaspoon almond extract

Combine above ingredients to spreading consistency. Drizzle over partially cooled butterhorns to make a breakfast or tea time treat.

For hors d'oeuvres, spread dough circles with smoked salmon and cream cheese or shredded sharp cheese, before rolling. As a flaky dinner roll, brush with melted butter prior to rolling.

Note: For larger butterhorns . . .cut circles into 10 wedges.

Blueberry Flannel Cakes

Serves: 4
Prepare: 10 min.

The title is misleading . . .beaten egg whites folded into the batter create a high, delicate pancake. Red raspberries substitute beautifully.

4 egg yolks
1 cup buttermilk*
1 cup flour
1 tablespoon sugar
½ teaspoon baking soda
½ teaspoon salt
4 egg whites
⅔ cup blueberries

In mixing bowl, beat egg yolks until thick. Add buttermilk *(or 1 cup whole milk mixed with 1 tablespoon vinegar). Sift together dry ingredients and stir into egg mixture. Beat egg whites until stiff, then fold into batter.

Drop by spoonfuls onto ungreased, hot griddle. Sprinkle a few blueberries on top of each cake. Brown both sides, turning only once.

Buttermilk Pancakes

Serves: 4   *These really are light as air!*
Prepare: 10 min.

3 eggs
2 cups buttermilk*
3 tablespoons melted butter
1½ cups flour
1 teaspoon baking powder
1 teaspoon baking soda
1 tablespoon sugar
½ teaspoon salt

In mixing bowl, beat eggs with a whisk until frothy, then add buttermilk and melted butter. Sift together dry ingredients, then blend in lightly but thoroughly. (Add a splash or two of regular milk, if you wish an even thinner pancake.) Ladle onto lightly greased, hot griddle and brown, turning only once.

Note: This batter keeps well in the refrigerator for several days. Stir before using. *Also, 2 cups milk mixed with 2 tablespoons vinegar may be substituted for the buttermilk.

German Oven Pancakes

Serves: 4 to 6
Prepare: 10 min.
Bake: 15 min.

Also known as "Auf Lauf", this may become your regular Sunday fare. The fruit and sundry garnishes make it a gorgeous repast with little effort.

1½ cups milk
1 cup flour
1 teaspoon sugar
6 eggs
Pinch of salt
4 ounces butter, melted

Preheat oven to 450°. In large bowl, blend milk into flour and sugar with a whisk. Lightly beat eggs with salt and whisk into milk and flour, blending well.

Pour melted butter into two 8-inch square baking dishes. Divide batter between dishes. Bake 15 minutes, or until it rises into big, golden brown puffs. (If "pancakes" brown too fast, lower temperature to 400°.)

Serve immediately with any or all of the following: fresh berries, peaches, fruit jam, sour cream, brown sugar or sugar, cinnamon, and applesauce.

Apple Pancake

Serves: 4
Prepare: 15 min.
Baking time: 10 min.

For a special breakfast or brunch, serve with
creamy scrambled eggs and crisp bacon.

2–4 cooking apples, cored
   and peeled
3 tablespoons sugar
1 teaspoon cinnamon
3 tablespoons butter
3 tablespoons flour
¼ teaspoon baking powder

Pinch of salt
3 tablespoons milk
2 egg yolks, lightly beaten
2 egg whites
3 tablespoons sugar
Sour cream

Preheat oven to 400°. Cut apples into ¼-inch thick slices. Combine sugar and cinnamon. Melt butter in a heavy, 10-inch skillet, and stir in sugar mixture. Neatly arrange apple slices in skillet and cook over medium heat for 5 minutes.

Combine flour, baking powder, and salt in a medium-size bowl. With a whisk, beat in milk and egg yolks. In a separate bowl, beat egg whites with 3 tablespoons sugar until they form soft peaks. Fold into flour mixture, then pour over apples.

Wrap a piece of foil around skillet handle and place in oven to bake for 10 minutes. Invert onto warm serving platter or serve out of skillet. Sour cream is perfect with this.

Sour Cream Coffee Cake

Serves: 10 to 12
Prepare: 20 min.
Bake: 1 hour

All those other sour cream coffee cake recipes, in all those other cookbooks, can not hold a candle to this one. Be sure to use only cake flour, but you may substitute margarine for the butter.

½ pound butter, softened
2 cups sugar
2 eggs
½ teaspoon vanilla
1 cup sour cream
1¾ cups sifted cake flour
1 teaspoon baking powder
¼ teaspoon salt
½ cup chopped pecans
   or walnuts
2 tablespoons dark
   brown sugar
1½ teaspoons cinnamon

Preheat oven to 350°. In large mixing bowl, cream together butter and sugar. Add eggs, one at a time, beating well after each addition, then add vanilla and sour cream. Sift together cake flour, baking powder, and salt. Stir into sour cream mixture.

Combine nuts, brown sugar, and cinnamon. Spoon half of batter into well-buttered tube pan. Sprinkle with half of nut mixture. Cover with rest of batter and then remaining nut mixture.

Bake at 350° for 1 hour. Cool in pan on rack. When completely cool, carefully remove cake from tube section so that it can be displayed, topping-end up, on cake plate.

Cranberry Coffee Cake

Serves: 12
Prepare: 20 min.
Bake: 50–60 min.

Wonderful any time of the year.

½ cup butter, softened
1 cup sugar
2 eggs
2 cups flour
1 teaspoon baking powder
½ teaspoon salt

1 cup sour cream
1 teaspoon almond extract
½ cup chopped walnuts
1 7-ounce can whole
   cranberry sauce

Preheat oven to 350°. Cream together butter and sugar. Add eggs, one at a time. Sift together flour, baking powder, and salt. Add to batter, alternating with sour cream. Stir in almond extract and nuts.

Grease and flour a tube pan. Pour in half of batter. With the back of a spoon, create a trough around center of batter. Carefully fill with cranberry sauce, so as not to reach sides. Top with remaining batter. Bake 50–60 minutes, until cake springs back to touch. Cool on rack.

¾ cup powdered sugar
½ teaspoon almond extract
2 tablespoons hot water
½ cup coarsely chopped
   walnuts

Combine powdered sugar, almond extract, and hot water. Pour over cooled cake as a glaze. Top with nuts.

Note: This cake is supposed to be on the heavy side, so do not use a bundt pan nor expect much rising.

Sherry Cake

Serves: 12
Prepare: 5 min.
Bake: 50 min.

A breeze of a recipe for meetings, to go with coffee or wine.

1 package yellow cake mix
1 4¾-ounce package
  instant vanilla pudding
1 teaspoon nutmeg
4 eggs
¾ cup sherry
¾ cup cooking oil

Preheat oven to 350°. In a large bowl, combine cake and pudding mixes and nutmeg. With a sturdy whisk or wooden spoon, combine remaining ingredients and mix into other. Pour into a greased angel food pan. Bake 50 minutes Invert to cool. Dust with powdered sugar. A good "keeper" for boating or backwoods excursions.

Desserts
and
Sweet Treats

Cream Cheese Cake(s)

Serves: 10 to 20
Prepare: 15 min.
Bake: 15 min. (10)
10 min. (5)

Here are two speedy desserts from one. The first version is with the popular graham cracker pie crust as an easy dinner party finale. Pass Blueberry Kir Sauce *to make it really special. The second is a transformation into mini-cheese cakes for buffet parties, luncheons, or tea time treats. Vanilla wafers are used in place of the graham cracker crust. Both desserts may be made a day ahead and refrigerated. They freeze well.*

1½ cups graham cracker
   crumbs
3 tablespoons sugar
¼ pound butter, melted

Preheat oven to 400°. Combine above ingredients and press into a 10-inch pie plate to form a crust. Bake 8–10 minutes. Cool.

2 8-ounce packages
   cream cheese, softened
3 eggs, beaten

¾–1 cup sugar
1 tablespoon lemon juice
1 teaspoon vanilla

Reduce oven temperature to 350°. Combine above ingredients until smooth. Pour into cooled crust. Bake for 15–20 minutes. Cool for 15 minutes.

1½ cups sour cream
¼ cup sugar
1½ teaspoons vanilla

24 vanilla wafers
(optional)

Combine and spoon onto cooled pie. Bake 350° for 10 minutes.
   To make 24 mini cheese cakes, place a vanilla wafer in each of 24 paper liners for miniature muffin tins. Place in tins and fill each ¾-full with cream cheese mixture. Bake at 350° for 10 minutes. Cool in tins, then top with sour cream mixture as you would the pie. Bake another 5 minutes.
   To serve, top each with a pretty berry or dollop of raspberry jam.

Blueberry Kir Sauce

Yield: 2 cups
Serves: 6 to 8
Prepare: 10 min.
Chill

...just as delicious as it sounds. Serve over vanilla ice cream or Cream Cheese Cake.

1 tablespoon cornstarch
½ cup Crème de Cassis
  (black currant liqueur)
¾ cup dry white wine
1 tablespoon lemon juice
1 tablespoon butter
1½ cups fresh or frozen
  blueberries

In a bowl, combine cornstarch and Cassis with a whisk, then add wine and lemon juice.

Melt butter in a medium saucepan and stir in wine mixture. Over medium heat, continue stirring until thick and glossy, then add berries. Stir until they burst. Chill.

Serve over ice cream. Whole strawberries and sprigs of mint are pretty garnishes.

Angel Lemon Delight

Serves: 6 to 8
Prepare: 20 min.
Bake: 40 min.

*A pudding-cake, this is refreshing and differ-
ent and easy. In fact, it's just plain wonderful!*

1 cup sugar
½ cup flour
¼ teaspoon salt
3 egg yolks
Juice and grated rind
   of 2 large lemons

2 tablespoons melted butter
1½ cups milk
3 egg whites
½ cup sugar

Preheat oven to 375°. Mix first 7 ingredients together in order given. Beat until very smooth and creamy.

Beat egg whites until stiff. Add ½ cup sugar and beat again. Fold into first set of ingredients. Pour into ungreased, shallow, 8×12-inch, glass baking dish. Set in a shallow roasting pan in 1-inch hot water. Bake, uncovered, for 40 minutes.

Serve warm or cold. It's pretty in shallow, glass bowls with stem strawberries on the side.

Russian Cream with Strawberries

Serves: 6
Prepare: 10 min.
Chill

The ideal light dessert that's very easy to make and yet still glamorous in appearance.

¾ cup sugar
1 envelope gelatin
½ cup water
1 cup heavy cream

1½ cups sour cream
1 teaspoon vanilla
Fresh or frozen strawberries

In a saucepan, combine sugar, gelatin, and water, mixing well. Let stand 5 minutes. Bring to a full boil, stirring constantly with a whisk. Remove from heat. Add heavy cream with a whisk.

In a large bowl, combine sour cream and vanilla. Gradually beat in hot mixture until smooth. Pour into an oiled, 4-cup mold, or into 6 or 8 individual molds or sherbet glasses. Chill.

To serve, top with fresh or frozen strawberries and decorate with chocolate curls or mint. Kirsch would be a delicious accent for the fruit.

Pears in Raspberry Sauce

Serves: 6
Prepare: 15 min.
Cook: 30 min.
Chill: 2 hours

There's a sophistication to this dessert that belies its ease of preparation. It may be made a day ahead, and is ideal for elegant but uncomplicated menus.

2 cups dry white wine
¾ cup sugar
Juice of 1 lemon
1 cup water
6 firm, ripe, flavorful pears

In a large, straight-sided sauce pan, bring to a boil the wine, sugar, lemon juice, and water. Cover and simmer while peeling pears. When preparing pears, leave stems intact but slice bottoms so that they will stand when served.

Drop pears into syrup. Cover and simmer until fruit is soft, about 20–30 minutes, turning occasionally with wooden spoons. Cool pears in syrup, then remove and drain about 5 minutes.

1 10-ounce package frozen
  raspberries, thawed
¼ cup sugar
Juice of ½ lemon
1 tablespoon orange liqueur

Puree above ingredients in a blender. Strain through a sieve to remove seeds. Pour sauce over pears and chill well.

To serve, stand pears upright in a pretty serving dish or individual bowls and top with sauce and sprigs of mint, if available. *Orange Ginger Cookies* are nice companions.

Frozen Peach Torte

Serves: 6 to 8
Prepare: 15 min.
Freeze

Perfect for hot summer evenings . . .easy to make in large quantities.

2 cups mashed
   fresh peaches
1½ tablespoons lemon juice
1 cup sugar

¾ cup heavy cream,
   whipped
1½ cups macaroon crumbs

This is another good recipe for a food processor. Mash enough sliced peaches to make 2 cups, adding lemon juice and sugar. Fold in whipped cream.

Crumble enough macaroons to make 1½ cups. Place half of them in bottom of an 8×8-inch square baking dish or ice tray. Pour in peach mixture. Top with remaining macaroon crumbs. Freeze until firm.

To serve, cut in wedges or squares. Slices of fresh peaches and sprigs of mint would be pretty decorations.

Fruit Pizza

Serves: 10 to 12
Prepare: 5 min.
Bake: 15 min.
Prepare: 15 min.
Chill: 2–3 hours

A great, big, beautiful dessert tart that everyone will love.

> ¾ cup butter, softened
> 1½ cups flour
> ½ cup powdered sugar

Preheat oven to 350°. Combine above ingredients (a food processor helps) and pat into a 12-inch pizza pan. Bake 15 minutes. Cool on rack.

> 1 8-ounce package cream
>   cheese, softened
> ¼ cup powdered sugar
> 1 teaspoon vanilla
> 1 quart fresh fruit*

Combine cream cheese, powdered sugar, and vanilla, and spread over cooled tart shell. On top of cheese, attractively arrange any combination of fruits: *strawberries, kiwi slices, blueberries, raspberries, sliced peaches, pineapple, grapes, cherries, etc.

> 3 tablespoons cornstarch
> ¼–½ cup sugar
> 1 cup fruit juice (pear,
>   pineapple, apple, or orange)
> 1 tablespoon lemon juice

Combine above ingredients in a saucepan, adjusting sugar quantity to sweetness of juice. Stir with a whisk over medium heat until thickened, but do not overcook. Immediately spoon over fruit to act as a glaze.

Refrigerate until ready to serve. Sprigs of mint would be a pretty garnish.

Linzertorte

Serves: 10 to 12
Prepare: 20 min.
Chill: 1 hour
Bake: 1 hour

This recipe was a favorite of the Von Trapp family of "Sound of Music" fame. It seems ideal for winter holiday menus and can be made a day or two ahead.

1 cup butter, softened
1 cup sugar
1 tablespoon grated lemon
  or orange peel
2 egg yolks
1½ cups flour
1 teaspoon baking powder
2 teaspoons cinnamon

½ teaspoon ground cloves
¼ teaspoon salt
1 cup ground filberts
  (hazelnuts), almonds,
  or walnuts
1 cup currant, plum, or
  loganberry preserves
Whipped cream

Cream together butter and sugar. Add grated peel, then egg yolks, one at a time, beating well.

Sift together flour, baking powder, spices, and salt. Stir into creamed mixture, then mix in nuts until thoroughly combined. Chill.

Preheat oven to 350°. Pat ⅔ of dough into 9-inch, removeable bottom, cake pan. Spread preserves over top. Roll out remaining dough (rechill, if it has become too soft), and cut into 8 strips about ¼-inch thick and ¾-inch wide. Place, lattice-fashion, on top of preserves, trimming at edges.

Bake 50–60 minutes, or until edges of strips recede from sides of pan. Cool. Cut into small wedges and garnish with whipped cream.

Apple Dumplings

Serves: 4
Prepare: 20 min.
Chill: 30 min.
Bake: 45 min.

We'll bet you've never had any like these! The caramel topping makes the difference.

1 pie crust recipe
   (see index)
4 whole baking apples,
   peeled and cored
4 tablespoons sugar
4 tablespoons butter

Nutmeg
1½ cups brown sugar
6 tablespoons water
Heavy cream
Dash of sherry (optional)

Prepare pie pastry and roll out on a floured pastry cloth into a square about ¼-inch thick. Cut into 4 squares. Place an apple on each square. Fill each apple with a tablespoon of sugar and a tablespoon of butter. Sprinkle with nutmeg. Mold pastry around each apple, sealing well. Arrange in ungreased baking dish and chill at least 30 minutes.

Preheat oven to 425°. Combine brown sugar and water, and simmer 5 minutes. Spoon 1 tablespoon of syrup over each dumpling and bake 10 minutes. Reduce temperature to 350°, and again baste each dumpling with a tablespoon of syrup. Continue baking another 30–40 minutes, basting at 10-minute intervals. Serve warm with heavy cream, flavored with a dash of sherry.

Odile's Apple Cake

Serves: 16
Prepare: 20 min.
Cook: 1 hour
Bake: 1½ hours

Very French, very easy, very good . . .you do need a 12-inch, removable bottom, tart pan, though. It's important for the "right look"!

4 pounds cooking apples,
    pared, cored,
    and quartered
½ cup sugar
Juice of ½ lemon
1–2 teaspoons vanilla

Combine above ingredients in a heavy pot or Dutch oven. Cover and simmer over low heat until apples are soft, about 30 minutes. Remove lid and continue cooking to reduce liquid, stirring frequently, until it becomes a thick applesauce (almost like apple butter); between 15–30 minutes. Cool.

8 ounces unsalted butter
1 cup sugar
3½ cups flour
4½ teaspoons baking
    powder
2 teaspoons almond extract

Preheat oven to 325°. Melt butter in a heavy pan. Stir in rest of ingredients and blend well. Using your fingers, mold ⅔ of this mixture into bottom and up sides of 12-inch tart pan.

Pour applesauce into crust and crumble remaining ⅓ of pastry over entire top. Bake 1½ hours or until top is brown and bubbly around rim. Cool cake in pan.

To serve, you may either invert onto platter and dust with powdered sugar for a finished, elegant look (candied violets would be a super touch), or leave crumb-face up to suit a brunch table.

Blackberry and Cream Pie

Serves: 8
Prepare: 20 min.
Bake: 40–50 min.

What would a Northwest summer be like without blackberries? This open-faced pie is a simple but special way to celebrate our beautiful month of August. Use your own pie crust recipe or try this particularly flaky version.

1½ cups flour
¾ teaspoon salt
⅔ cup vegetable shortening
3 tablespoons cold water

Sift together flour and salt into a mixing bowl. Remove ¼ cup to a smaller bowl. Cut shortening into larger bowl until size of small peas. With a fork, combine cold water and reserved ¼ cup of flour until a smooth paste. Stir into shortening and flour, combining well.

Because this is a very tender pastry, it's best to roll it out on a lightly floured pastry cloth with a cloth-covered rolling pin. Line a 9½ to 10-inch glass pie plate with pastry (there will be some excess). Preheat oven to 425°.

4–5 cups blackberries,
   gently washed
   and drained
1 teaspoon lemon juice
   (optional)

1 cup sour cream
½ cup brown sugar
1 tablespoon flour
Heavy cream

Place well-drained berries in pie shell, sprinkling with lemon juice (omit if berries are tart). Combine sour cream, brown sugar, and flour. Spread over berries.

Bake at 425° for 10 minutes. Reduce heat to 325°. Bake at least 30–40 minutes more, or until berries are soft, juicy, and bubbling. Serve while pie is still warm, passing a pitcher of heavy cream.

Wild Blackberry Cobbler

Serves: 6 to 8
Prepare: 15 min.
Bake: 50 min.

It's such fun to discover and pick the first berries of the season, and bring them in, firm and glistening, to decorate your kitchen counter. If you've already had a few orgies of berries and cream, this is a delicious diversion.

1 cup sugar
1 tablespoon cornstarch
¾ cup water

6 cups blackberries, gently washed and drained
2 tablespoons butter

Preheat oven to 400°. Combine sugar, cornstarch, and water. Stir into berries then pour into ungreased, shallow, 9×11-inch baking dish. Dot with butter. Bake, uncovered, at 400° for 20 minutes or until bubbling.

1 cup flour
1 tablespoon sugar
2 teaspoons baking powder
½ teaspoon salt

¼ cup shortening
½ cup (on the generous side!) sour cream
Heavy cream

Combine and sift dry ingredients into a mixing bowl. Cut in shortening until it resembles fine crumbs. Stir in sour cream with a fork until well mixed.

Drop dough by spoonfuls on top of bubbling fruit. Bake another 30 minutes, until biscuits are browned. Serve in bowls with cream.

Lemon Pie

Serves: 8
Prepare: 15 min.
Cool: 15 min.
Bake: 5 min.

We've never made or tasted a lemon pie like this one. It's easy and wonderful.

4 egg yolks
½ cup sugar
1 tablespoon water
Juice and rind of 1 lemon

4 egg whites
½ cup sugar
1 9-inch pie shell, baked

In top of double boiler, beat egg yolks with sugar until light-colored. Add water, lemon juice and rind. Place over boiling water and stir constantly with a whisk until thick; about 3–5 minutes. Remove and cool, stirring occasionally.

Preheat oven to 400°. In a separate bowl, beat egg whites until they form soft mounds. Gradually beat in sugar. Continue beating until stiff peaks are formed.

Blend half of beaten egg whites into cooled lemon mixture. Pour into baked pie shell. Gently spread rest of meringue over top, making sure it touches crust everywhere to prevent shrinkage. Swirl into pretty peaks.

Bake at 400°–425° until meringue is lightly browned, about 5 minutes. Dessert may sit on counter for several hours before serving.

Orange Sherbet Pie

Serves: 8 to 10
Prepare: 20 min.
Freeze

So pretty and refreshing.

6 tablespoons butter
1 7-ounce package flaked
   coconut
½ gallon orange sherbet,
   softened

¼ cup orange liqueur
   (Triple Sec or Cointreau)
Sprigs of mint
Mandarin orange segments
Zests of orange peel

In large, heavy skillet, melt butter over medium heat. Add coconut and stir constantly until golden, about 6 to 7 minutes. Remove from heat.

Press browned coconut into 9-inch pie plate to form a crust up to brim, reserving 2 tablespoons of the coconut flakes for garnish. Spread half of sherbet over crust. Drizzle with liqueur, then spread in rest of sherbet, mounding top attractively. Sprinkle with reserved coconut. Freeze 2–3 hours or overnight.

Let stand 10–15 minutes before serving. Garnish with mint sprigs, orange segments, and zests of orange peel.

Frozen Pumpkin Pie

Serves: 6 to 8
Prepare: 15 min.
Bake: 5 min.
Freeze: overnight

This is a super autumn dessert. If you have a food processor, it will take you only a few minutes to prepare.

1 4-ounce package pecans,
  ground
½ cup ground ginger snaps
¼ cup sugar
¼ cup butter, softened

Preheat oven to 450°. Combine the 4 ingredients and press into 9-inch pie plate to form a crust. Bake 5–7 minutes. Cool.

1 cup canned pumpkin
½ cup brown sugar, packed
½ teaspoon ginger
½ teaspoon cinnamon

¼ teaspoon nutmeg
½ teaspoon salt
1 quart vanilla ice cream,
  softened

Combine pumpkin, sugar, spices, and salt, and beat several minutes. Stir in ice cream and pour into cooled crust. Freeze completely. Remove from freezer 15 minutes before serving. You may top with whipped cream and chocolate curls, if you wish.

French Silk Chocolate Pie

Serves: 6
Prepare: 15 min.
Chill: 2–3 hours

Deceptively light, yet luscious.

½ cup butter, softened
¾ cup sugar
2 eggs
1 square semi-sweet
  chocolate, melted

1 teaspoon vanilla
1 9-inch pie crust,
  baked and cooled

Cream together butter and sugar. Add eggs, one at a time, beating 5 minutes per egg. Add melted (but not hot) chocolate and vanilla. Pour into baked pie crust. Chill several hours.

1 cup heavy cream
½ cup powdered sugar
1 tablespoon cocoa

½ teaspoon vanilla
Toasted sliced almonds
Chocolate shavings

Before serving, whip together cream, powdered sugar, cocoa, and vanilla into soft peaks. Spoon onto pie and sprinkle with toasted almonds and shavings of chocolate.

Kahlua Mousse

Serves: 6
Prepare: 10 min.
Chill: 1 hour, plus

Velvety and delicious.

1 6-ounce package semi-
   sweet chocolate chips
⅓ cup hot coffee
4 egg yolks
2 tablespoons Kahlua
   liqueur

4 egg whites
2 tablespoons sugar
Whipped cream
Chocolate curls

Place chocolate chips and hot coffee in electric blender and blend at high speed for 30 seconds, or until smooth. Add egg yolks and Kahlua. Blend another 30 seconds.

In medium-size bowl, beat egg whites until foamy and about double in volume. Gradually beat in sugar until well-blended. Fold in chocolate mixture until there are no streaks of whites.

Spoon into 6 parfait or wine glasses. Chill at least 1 hour before serving. Garnish with whipped cream and chocolate curls.

Westhaven Cake

Serves: 10 to 12
Prepare: 20 min.
Bake: 30–35 min.

The dates contribute to the moist, flavorful virtues of this dessert without letting you know they are there.

1 8-ounce package
  chopped dates
1 cup boiling water
1 teaspoon baking soda
½ cup butter, softened
1 cup sugar

2 eggs
1¾ cups flour
½ teaspoon salt
¼ cup cocoa
1 teaspoon vanilla

Preheat oven to 350°. In a small bowl, cover dates with boiling water and let stand until cool. Then stir in baking soda.

In large mixing bowl, cream together butter and sugar. Add remaining ingredients, including cooled date mixture (don't forget the baking soda), blending well.

1 6-ounce package
  chocolate chips
½ cup chopped walnuts
  or pecans
Powdered sugar (optional)

Pour batter into greased, shallow, 8×12-inch baking dish.* Sprinkle chocolate chips and nuts over top. Bake at 350° for 30–35 minutes. Sprinkle with powdered sugar while still hot. Leave in pan to cool and serve.

Note: You may use a 9×13-inch baking dish but cake will not be so high. Reduce baking time by 5 minutes.

Chocolate Mocha Blitz Torte

Serves: 8 to 10
Prepare: 30 min.
Bake: 35–40 min.
Cool

There are no words to describe.

2 ounces German sweet
  chocolate
¼ cup boiling water
½ cup butter, softened
1 cup sugar
2 egg yolks

1 teaspoon vanilla
1¼ cups sifted cake flour
¼ teaspoon salt
½ teaspoon baking soda
½ cup buttermilk
2 egg whites, stiffly beaten

Preheat oven to 325°. Melt chocolate in boiling water and cool. Grease and flour two 9 or 10-inch cake pans with removable bottoms.

In large mixing bowl, cream butter and sugar until fluffy. Add egg yolks, one at a time, beating well. Add cooled chocolate and vanilla. Sift together flour, salt, and baking soda. Add to chocolate mixture, alternating with buttermilk, beating well with each addition. Fold in beaten egg whites. Divide between cake pans.

3 egg whites
¾ cup sugar
1 cup lightly toasted,
  slivered almonds

Beat egg whites until they form soft mounds. Gradually beat in sugar. When stiff peaks are formed, spread meringue over batter. Sprinkle with toasted almonds. Bake at 325° for 35–40 minutes, or until an inserted toothpick tests clean. Cool on racks.

1 cup heavy cream
1 teaspoon instant coffee
  granules
¼ cup powdered sugar

When cakes are completely cool, whip cream, adding coffee granules and powdered sugar. Spread between layers and refrigerate until serving.

Pots de Crème

Serves: 4
Prepare: 10 min.
Chill: 1 hour

*Geared for a blender, this recipe is the perfect
spur-of-the moment dessert, and yet is quite
sophisticated. If doubling, be sure to do it in
two batches.*

1 6-ounce package semi-
    sweet chocolate chips
1 egg
1 teaspoon sugar
1 teaspoon vanilla
¾ cup scalded milk

Place first 4 ingredients in blender. Cover, turn on to high, then
slowly add near-boiling milk. Continue to blend at high speed for 2
minutes.

Pour into 4 pot de crème pots or wine glasses. Chill until set.
We've served these on glass plates with sprigs of mint and whole
strawberries or raspberries. Beautiful!

159

Chocolate Whiskey Cake

Serves: 10 to 12
Prepare: 20 min.
Steep: 2–3 hours
Bake: 20–25 min.

*For those who adore chocolate, this is a must.
It's a small but powerfully rich and delicious
dessert, in which the softened raisins and the
liquor are quite subtle.*

¼ cup raisins
¼ cup whiskey
½ teaspoon almond extract

Combine the above ingredients. Cover and steep several hours or
overnight.

8 ounces dark sweet
   chocolate
3 tablespoons water
4 ounces unsalted butter,
   softened
6 egg yolks
½ cup sugar

⅓ cup cake flour
½ cup ground almonds
6 egg whites
Pinch of salt
¼ teaspoon cream of tartar
2½ tablespoons sugar

Preheat oven to 375°. Break chocolate into small chunks. Place in
top of double boiler with 3 tablespoons water. Melt over simmering
water. With a whisk, add softened butter gradually, stirring until
smooth. Cool.

Butter and flour one 8-inch, round, removable bottom, cake
pan. Beat egg yolks and ½ cup sugar until pale yellow and creamy.
Beat in cooled chocolate mixture, flour, and ground almonds. Stir
in raisins and whiskey.

In a separate bowl, beat egg whites with salt until foamy. Add
cream of tartar and beat until soft peaks are formed. Gradually add
2½ tablespoons sugar, beating until peaks are firm and glossy.
Stir ⅓ of beaten whites into chocolate batter to lighten it. Fold in
remaining whites quickly but gently with a rubber spatula. Turn
into prepared pan.

Bake at 375° for 20–25 minutes, but do not overbake. Cake should have pulled away from sides and be firm in center, but still moist. Cool in pan on a rack.

6 ounces dark sweet chocolate, broken in chunks

4 ounces unsalted butter
½ tablespoon corn syrup
½ teaspoon salad oil

Melt chocolate with rest of ingredients in double boiler, stirring until smooth. Cool until almost set then spread as a thick glaze over cooled cake, letting it run down sides.

Birthday Confection Cake

Serves: 10
Prepare: 10 min.

Desperate for a birthday cake? The baker forgot your order, or you've been caught in another unbearable traffic jam? Here's a beautiful solution.

1 baked angel food cake, cooled
3 cups heavy cream
3–4 packets instant hot cocoa mix (milk chocolate)
⅔ cup chopped almonds, toasted

With a serrated knife, slice off 1 inch of top of cake and set aside. Continuing to use bread knife, slice out a trough around the center of cake, about 1 inch in from both inner and outer edges, to within 1 inch of bottom.

Beat cream until thickened, then gradually beat in 3 to 4 instant cocoa packets, according to taste. Continue beating until stiff. Fold in half of chopped nuts. Spoon into cake cavity until filled. Replace top of cake. Frost cake with remaining whipped cream mixture. Sprinkle with rest of almonds.

If not serving within a half hour or so, chill. It will keep nicely all day in refrigerator.

Sherry Bars

Serves: 12 to 50!
Prepare: 20 min.
Bake: 30–40 min.
Chill

Extremely rich, with a fudge brownie bottom and creamy filling, they can become a glorious company dessert by topping with whipped cream and chocolate shavings, or vanilla ice cream and chopped pecans.

4 ounces unsweetened chocolate	2 cups sugar
1 cup butter	½ teaspoon salt
4 eggs	1 cup flour
	1 teaspoon vanilla

Preheat oven to 325°. Melt chocolate and butter. Cool.

Beat eggs. Add sugar, salt, and cooled chocolate mixture. Stir in flour and vanilla. Pour into a greased and floured, 9×13-inch, shallow baking dish. Bake 30–40 minutes, until it springs back to touch. Cool.

½ cup butter, melted	1 cup chopped pecans
1 pound powdered sugar	¼ cup pale dry sherry
¼ cup heavy cream	(not cooking sherry)

Beat all together and spread over cooled chocolate layer. Chill.

6 ounces semi-sweet chocolate chips
4 tablespoons butter
3 tablespoons water

Combine and heat above ingredients to melt. Spread over chilled layers. Re-chill, or serve at room temperature. Cut in 1 to 2-inch squares to serve as holiday candy-cookie treats, or in 3-inch squares for dessert with any of the suggested toppings.

Apricot Bars

Yield: 32
Prepare: 25 min.
Bake: 25 min.
    30 min.

We put these on equal footing with Lemon Bars.

½ cup butter, softened
¼ cup sugar
1 cup flour

Preheat oven to 350°. Combine butter, sugar, and flour until crumbly. Press into bottom of greased, 8-inch square baking pan. Bake 25 minutes.

⅔ cup dried apricots, rinsed
⅓ cup flour
½ teaspoon baking powder
¼ teaspoon salt
2 eggs

1 cup light brown sugar, firmly packed
½ teaspoon brandy flavoring (optional)
½ cup chopped walnuts

In a sauce pan, cover apricots with water and simmer 10 minutes. Drain, cool, and coarsely chop.

Sift together flour, baking powder, and salt. Beat eggs, then gradually beat in brown sugar. Stir in flour mixture, flavoring, nuts, and chopped apricots.

Spread apricot mixture over baked crust. Return to oven for another 30 minutes. Cool in pan before cutting into 1×2-inch bars.

Lemon Bars

Yield: 3–4 dozen
Prepare: 20 min.
Bake: 20 min.
     20 min.

We almost made the mistake of assuming that this was the same recipe that has been quite popular the last few years. This one came from Norway via an 80-year-old dear friend. There are just enough variations to make it just that much better!

2 cups sifted flour
1 cup butter, softened
½ cup sifted powdered
   sugar

Preheat oven to 325°. Mix the above ingredients together well. Pack into 10×14-inch, ungreased, baking dish. Bake 20 minutes.

4 eggs
2 cups sugar
6 tablespoons lemon juice
2 teaspoons grated
   lemon rind

¼ cup flour
¼ teaspoon baking powder
¼ teaspoon salt
Powdered sugar

In mixing bowl, beat eggs lightly. Add sugar, lemon juice and rind. Sift together flour, baking powder, and salt. Beat into egg mixture by hand. Pour over cookie layer as soon as it comes from oven.

Increase oven temperature to 350°. Bake another 20 minutes, until done. Sprinkle with powdered sugar, cool, then cut into squares.

Chocolate Chip Peanut Butter Cookies

Yield: 7 dozen
Prepare: 10 min.
Bake: 15 min.

These are wonderful! When packed in a "care" package, they smelled so good that they prompted the UPS agent to beg for the recipe!

1 cup butter, softened
1 cup sugar
1 cup brown sugar
2 eggs
1 cup chunk-style peanut butter

2 cups flour
1 teaspoon baking soda
1 12-ounce package semi-sweet chocolate chips

Preheat oven to 350°. Cream together butter and sugars. Beat eggs in well, then peanut butter. Sift together flour and baking soda; add to batter, mixing well. Fold in chocolate chips.

Drop by teaspoonfuls onto ungreased baking sheet. Bake 12–15 minutes. When done, centers should still be slightly soft.

Chocolate-topped Oatmeal Cookies

Yield: 5 dozen
Prepare: 10 min.
Bake: 25–30 min.

They have a nice "almond roca" look and taste. Yummy!

1 cup butter, softened
½ cup light brown sugar
½ cup granulated sugar

2 egg yolks
1 cup flour
1 cup oatmeal

Preheat oven to 350°. Cream together butter and sugar. Beat in yolks; add flour and oatmeal. This makes a thick, heavy batter, so use fingers to spread out into well-greased, 9×13-inch baking dish. Bake 25–30 minutes. Cool.

1 8-ounce bar of milk
  chocolate
2 tablespoons butter
½ cup chopped almonds,
  toasted

Melt chocolate bar with butter. Spread over cooled cookie layer. Sprinkle with nuts. Cool and cut into 1½-inch squares. These freeze well.

Mrs. Overlake's Cookies

Yield: 27 big cookies!
Prepare: 10 min.
Bake: 15 min.

The secret is to overdose on chocolate chips and nuts, then underbake for a chewy, moist, scrumptious cookie.

1 cup butter, melted
¾ cup sugar
¾ cup brown sugar
2 eggs
1 overflowing teaspoon
  vanilla

2½ cups unsifted flour
1 teaspoon baking soda
1 teaspoon salt
3–4 cups (18–24 ounces)
  chocolate chips
2 cups chopped pecans

Preheat oven to 325°. In a large bowl, cream together butter and sugars, then beat in eggs and vanilla. Sift together flour, baking soda, and salt. Stir into butter mixture, forming a stiff batter. Add chips and nuts.

Use an ice cream scoop to drop batter on ungreased cookie sheet, averaging 9 cookies per sheet. Bake at 325° for 15–18 minutes, checking periodically to see that they are not overbaked.

American Crisp Cookies

Yield: 80
Prepare: 15 min.
Bake: 6–8 min.

You may recognize these as "Ranger Cookies" or "World's Best" or whatever, but teenagers call them "Awesome"!

1 cup butter, softened
1 cup sugar
1 cup brown sugar, packed
1 cup oil
1 egg, beaten
3½ cups flour
1 teaspoon salt

1 teaspoon baking soda
1 cup corn flakes
1 cup regular oatmeal
½ cup shredded coconut
1 tablespoon sour cream
2 teaspoons vanilla

Preheat oven to 350°. In a large mixing bowl, cream together butter and sugars. Beat in oil and egg. Sift flour with salt and baking soda, and add to batter. Combine well with remaining ingredients.

Using one level tablespoonful at a time, drop on ungreased cookie sheets. Flatten with a fork. Bake at 350° for 6–8 minutes. Cool a few minutes before removing.

Brown Sugar Chews

Yield: 5 dozen
Prepare: 10 min.
Bake: 20 min.

They are like delicious butterscotch brownies without the butter, and painless to make. The kids will love them.

1 cup flour
1 teaspoon baking powder
2 cups brown sugar
  (do not pack)

2 eggs
1 tablespoon vanilla
1 cup walnuts

Preheat oven to 350°. Sift flour and baking powder. Combine in a bowl with brown sugar. Lightly beat eggs with a fork. Add to rest with vanilla. Stir in nuts and pour into greased, shallow 9×13-inch baking pan.

Bake 20–25 minutes, until slightly brown edge is just beginning to pull away. Do not overbake. Completely cool on rack before cutting into squares.

Our donor found this recipe in an American Legion Auxiliary cookbook from the old mining town of Downieville, California. She says that they are good "keepers", if you hide them!

Orange Ginger Cookies

Yield: 6 dozen
Prepare: 10 min.
Chill: 3 hours plus
Bake: 5 min.

A light, crisp cookie that can "finish-off" ice cream, fruits, or pudding desserts . . .just right with coffee.

1 cup butter, softened
1½ cups sugar
1 egg
2 tablespoons light
  corn syrup
3 cups flour
2 teaspoons baking soda

2 teaspoons cinnamon
2 teaspoons powdered
  ginger
½ teaspoon ground cloves
1 tablespoon shredded
  orange peel

Cream butter and sugar. Beat in egg and corn syrup. Sift together dry ingredients. Stir into batter along with orange peel. Shape into two 9-inch long rolls, about 2 inches wide. Wrap in waxed paper or plastic wrap and chill several hours or overnight.

Preheat oven to 400°. Slice rolls ⅛-inch thick. Place 2 inches apart on ungreased cookie sheets. Bake 5–6 minutes, until light brown. While still warm, sprinkle with granulated sugar.

Fudge Brownies

Yield: 2 dozen
Prepare: 10 min.
Bake: 35 min.

A great favorite at Overlake for years, these are wonderfully "fudgie".

1 cup butter, softened
2 cups sugar
2 teaspoons vanilla
4 eggs
4 1-ounce squares
   unsweetened chocolate,
   melted

1 cup sifted flour
1 cup chopped walnuts
   (optional)

Preheat oven to 325°. Cream butter, sugar, and vanilla. Beat in eggs. Blend in chocolate. Stir in flour and nuts.

   Pour into greased, 9×13-inch baking pan. Bake until dry on top and just beginning to crack, but still soft to touch; about 35 minutes.

Chocolate Butter Balls

Yield: 7 to 8 dozen
Prepare: 30 min.

A beautiful Christmas treat for teachers and friends.

1 cup peanut butter
1 cup chopped nuts
1 cup powdered sugar
1 cup chopped dates

1 12-ounce package
   chocolate chips
2 tablespoons paraffin
   shavings, packed

Mix peanut butter, nuts, powdered sugar, and dates together, well. Roll into small balls, about ¾-inch in diameter.

   Melt chocolate chips and paraffin in double boiler. Dip balls in chocolate to coat. Place on waxed paper to cool and harden. If chocolate becomes too stiff to work with, reheat. These will keep nicely in the fridge for at least a month.

Freezer Mints

Yield: 1¼ pounds
Prepare: 15 min.
Chill or freeze

"When I was a child, a big bowl and a wooden spoon for stirring these treats kept me happy for hours in my mother's holiday kitchen. A food processor now makes these a breeze . . .it seems a shame!"

1 1-pound box
  powdered sugar
¼ pound butter, softened
Peppermint flavoring to taste
2 tablespoons cream
  (conditional)
Food coloring (optional)

In food processor, cream butter then add sugar in batches. When mixture is crumbly, add peppermint flavoring and process. Continue adding rest of sugar. Add cream *only* if necessary. Mixture must be very stiff. Add food coloring, if desired.

Form small balls and place on waxed paper. Flatten with a fork dipped in powdered sugar to prevent sticking. Cover and store indefinitely in freezer.

Note: You might have fun varying the flavoring; i.e. rum, orange, vanilla, almond, lemon, etc.

Vreni's Alcoholic Cherries

Distill: 6 weeks

"This recipe was given to me by Vreni Buttiker, a Swiss friend who lived next door to us in Paris. In late fall or early winter, the crock would appear at her tea table. We would nibble on the cherries, then succumb to a glass of the 'juice'. I usually get these picked and under way by late August or early September. By Christmas, they are ready for bottling in pretty gift containers for 'initiated' friends who have christened them, 'Cherry Bombs'!"

Tart cherries*
Sugar cubes
Brandy or vodka
Cinnamon stick (optional)
Large crock or glass
    container
One cool, dark place

Stem, but do not pit cherries. Fill crock ¾-full with cherries. Fill remainder with sugar cubes. Pour brandy or vodka over to cover all. A cinnamon stick may be added, if you wish. Cover crock tightly and let sit at least 6 weeks in a cool, dark place.

*Sweet cherries may be used, but cut way back on the sugar.

Index